POSITION CLASSIFICATION AND

SALARY ADMINISTRATION IN LIBRARIES

POSITION CLASSIFICATION AND

SALARY ADMINISTRATION IN LIBRARIES

*****

Prepared by the
Subcommittee on Job Analysis Manual and
Classification and Pay Plan Manual
of the
A.L.A. Board on Personnel Administration

*****

CHICAGO

AMERICAN LIBRARY ASSOCIATION

1951

PERSONNEL OF THE

SUBCOMMITTEE ON JOB ANALYSIS MANUAL AND

CLASSIFICATION AND PAY PLAN MANUAL

OF THE

A.L.A. BOARD ON PERSONNEL ADMINISTRATION

Marian McFadden, Chairman

Advisory Group

Harold F. Brigham   Robert Alexander Miller
Esther Virginia Burrin   Ralph Day Remley
          Hazel Beatrice Warren

Working Group

Bertha Ashby   Pauline French
Miriam Atkinson   Mary Louise Hodapp
Catherine Bailey   Helen L. Norris
Mrs. Naomi Barnett Blair   Mrs. Martha Eckert Schaaf
Margaret Louise Donnell   Mrs. Florence Buenting Schad

Copyright 1951 by the American Library Association

PREFACE

This manual has been written to provide a practical step-by-step guide to position classification and salary administration for the use of administrators, staff, and governing boards of libraries interested in developing such plans. The study has come out of an expressed need for such a tool, as librarians have become increasingly aware of the advantages of a classification of positions, of the importance of a job analysis as a basis for this classification, and of the place of classification in setting up and administering an equitable salary schedule. The manual has been planned with libraries of all types and sizes in mind but has been geared primarily to the medium-sized public library, with a staff of 10 or more. Where variations would occur, however, additional examples have been added for libraries of different sizes and types.

There is no doubt that the establishment of a sound position-classification plan for any organization can best be accomplished by engaging the services of a professional personnel consultant or firm to do the job. This not only insures complete objectivity, but the resulting plan will also bear the mark of authority. Moreover, such experts can bring to the solution of the many technical problems arising in a position-classification survey a broad understanding of good personnel theory and practice not likely to be found in a group whose training and experience have been mainly in the field of librarianship. If such help cannot be financed for the entire project, this service should at least be sought at the beginning of the survey for advice in procedure and, if possible, for the actual classifying of positions.

All libraries undertaking such a project, however, will wish to understand the techniques involved. Many will wish to do all the preparatory work, under the direction of the experts, calling on them only to finish the survey. Some will be forced to do the entire job themselves. This manual, therefore, attempts to answer the questions: How can we prepare for or carry through, if necessary, a position-classification survey? How can we prepare a salary schedule based on the resulting plan? and, How can we install and administer such plans?

Position classification is not a procedure which is done once and for all time. As positions change they must be reanalyzed and reclassified in order to keep the plan current. In any organization constant changes are being made in work methods and individual assignments; consequently, a periodic analysis is necessary if a true picture of the whole is to be maintained. Thus, this manual is designed as a guide not only in establishing a position-classification and pay plan, but also as a tool for its continued maintenance.

The techniques presented herein are not original. They have been adapted from established and tested methods used in government, business, and industry. Although the methods used in certain library analyses have been studied, no comparison of these methods is made. The techniques presented are workable in a library analysis and have been tested in libraries previous to and during the writing of this manual. The subcommittee has drawn heavily on the publication,

Position-classification in the Public Service,[1] and on the A.L.A. series on classification and pay plans for libraries,[2] and recommends that any library undertaking a survey make use of these basic tools.

The subcommittee is grateful to the Civil Service Assembly of the United States and Canada, the University of Chicago Press, and the American Library Association for permission to use material from their publications.

                                        Marian McFadden, Chairman
                                        Subcommittee on Job Analysis Manual
                                        and Classification and Pay Plan Manual

---

[1] Civil Service Assembly of the United States and Canada, Committee on Position-classification and Pay Plans in the Public Service, Position-classification in the Public Service (Chicago: The Assembly, 1941)

[2] American Library Association, Board on Personnel Administration, Classification and Pay Plans for Municipal Public Libraries (Chicago: American Library Assn., 1939)

American Library Association, Board on Personnel Administration, Subcommittee on Budgets, Compensation and Schemes of Service for Libraries Connected with Universities, Colleges and Teacher Training Institutions, Classification and Pay Plans for Libraries in Institutions of Higher Education (2d ed.; Chicago: American Library Assn., 1947), 3v.

CONTENTS

	Page
PREFACE	v
Chapter I – MEANING OF TERMS	1
Position Classification	1
Job Analysis	2
Time Study	2
Job Description	2
Job Specification	2
Position	2
Classes of Positions	3
Class Title	3
Class Definition	3
Class Specification	3
Classification Grades	3
Services	3
Salary Schedule	4
Salary Increments	4
Chapter II – PRELIMINARY PLANNING	5
Presenting the Idea to Those Concerned	5
Selecting the Agency to Do the Work	5
Outside agencies; Personnel departments; Employee committees; Qualifications of the analysts; Number of analysts needed	
Deciding What Positions Are to Be Included in the Survey	7
Selecting the Method	7
The questionnaire; The interview; Direct observation; Combination of the three methods	
Assembling and Studying the Necessary Tools	8
Chapter III – CONDUCTING THE JOB ANALYSIS	10
Preparing the Job Analysis Questionnaire	10
Identifying data; Who fills out the form; How the tasks are listed and described; The time spent on tasks; Indication of supervision	
Preparing Instructions for Employees	11
Making Arrangements with Supervisors	12
Explaining the Survey Plans to Employees	12
Distributing and Returning the Questionnaires	13
Arranging and Studying Questionnaires	13
Writing Job Descriptions	13
The job title; The job summary; The work performed	
Conducting Interviews	14
Writing Job Specifications	16
Chapter IV – FACTORS TO BE CONSIDERED IN CLASSIFYING POSITIONS	18
Difficulty and Complexity of Duties	18
How far work has progressed; How work is assigned; Procedure followed by the employee; Relationship of one employee's work to others; Variety and scope of duties	
Nonsupervisory Responsibilities	20
Independence of action and decision; Responsibility for	

	Page
recommending plans and policies; Responsibility for money, supplies, equipment; Responsibility for accuracy; Responsibility for public contacts	
Supervisory and Administrative Responsibilities	23
Policies; Planning; Flow of work; "Housekeeping" management; Review of work; Assignments; Work methods; Coordination; Production; The limitation of initiative; The number and types of positions supervised; The level of difficulty and variety of functions supervised	
Qualification Standards	25

Chapter V – DEVELOPING THE SCHEDULE OF CLASSES ... 27
   Analyzing Positions ... 27
      Professional positions; Nonprofessional positions; The levels of responsibility
   Determining Classes ... 28
   Selecting Class Titles ... 30
   Writing Class Definitions ... 30
   Setting up Classification Grades ... 31
   Making Known to Employees the Tentative Classification Grades, Class Titles, and Definitions ... 32

Chapter VI – ALLOCATING POSITIONS TO SPECIFIC CLASSES ... 33
   Tentatively Allocating Positions to Classes ... 33
      Mixed positions; Position comparisons; A final check on allocations
   Writing Class Specifications ... 38
      Typical tasks; Minimum qualifications
   Reviewing and Publishing Class Specifications ... 39
   Notifying Employees of Allocations ... 40
   Adjusting Disagreements ... 40
   Adopting the Position-classification Plan ... 40

Chapter VII – INSTALLATION AND ADMINISTRATION OF THE POSITION-CLASSIFICATION PLAN ... 42
   Using the Plan in Administration ... 42
      Pay plans and salary budgets; A personnel tool; Planning and improving organization; Employee-management relations
   Providing for the Installation and Administration of the Plan ... 43
      The agency to administer the plan; Rules for the installation and administration of the plan
   Problems Involved in Adapting a New Plan to an Existing One ... 44
      The salary problem; The qualification problem; The rank or prestige problem
   Keeping the Plan Current ... 46
      Reclassification procedure; Periodic review

Chapter VIII – SALARY SCHEDULING ... 48
   Selecting the Agency ... 48
   Factors in Setting a Salary Schedule ... 48
      Difficulty, responsibilities, and qualification requirements of

	Page
the work; Rates of competing employers; Standards set by library and related associations; Economic and social conditions; Ability of the jurisdiction to pay	
The Mechanics of Setting a Salary Schedule.	50
Setting a rate for key positions; Setting rates for other positions with respect to key positions; Establishing salary ranges for each grade; Providing for a career service; Providing for cost-of-living adjustments	
Adopting the Salary Schedule.	55
Placing the Classified Positions on the Scale	55
Administering the Salary Schedule	56
Keeping the Salary Schedule Current	57

SUMMARY OF STEPS INVOLVED IN A POSITION-CLASSIFICATION AND SALARY-ADMINISTRATION SURVEY 59

SELECTED BIBLIOGRAPHY. 61

Appendixes
- A. JOB ANALYSIS QUESTIONNAIRE. 63
- B. DAILY WORK SHEET - DESK ASSISTANT 65
- C. DAILY WORK SHEET - CHIEF, CIRCULATION DEPARTMENT. 66
- D. SAMPLE INSTRUCTIONS 67
- E. COMPLETED JOB ANALYSIS QUESTIONNAIRE - DESK ASSISTANT 70
- F. COMPLETED JOB ANALYSIS QUESTIONNAIRE - CHIEF, CIRCULATION DEPARTMENT 72
- G. COMPLETED JOB ANALYSIS QUESTIONNAIRE - JUNIOR REFERENCE LIBRARIAN 74
- H. SAMPLE JOB DESCRIPTION - DESK ASSISTANT 76
- I. SAMPLE JOB DESCRIPTION - CHIEF, CIRCULATION DEPARTMENT. 77
- J. SAMPLE JOB DESCRIPTION - JUNIOR REFERENCE LIBRARIAN 78
- K. SAMPLE CLASS SPECIFICATION - CHIEF CIRCULATION LIBRARIAN. 79
- L. SAMPLE CLASS SPECIFICATION - INTERMEDIATE REFERENCE LIBRARIAN . . 81

Chapter I

MEANING OF TERMS

Position Classification

Classification is the arrangement of units into groups on the basis of certain distinguishing characteristics. A classification of positions is a grouping of positions into classes based on the similarity of: (1) the nature and difficulty of work performed; (2) the amount and level of responsibility involved; and (3) the experience and training required for the proper performance of the duties of the position. Librarians should recognize the possibility of classifying positions, for they work daily with the classification of knowledge for the purpose of arranging books. In a similar way they should be able to classify or group the collective duties of one position in relation to those of another.

One of the underlying assumptions of position classification is that it can be done with a reasonable degree of objectivity. Since it is difficult to disassociate jobs from the persons holding them, it is inevitable that some subjective elements will creep into such an undertaking, but certain safeguards can be employed to insure an objective approach. First is the selection of one or more individuals who have some knowledge of the positions to be classified and can view them impartially. A second safeguard is to establish clearly the factors which differentiate the jobs as to degree of difficulty and responsibility. Finally, several appraisals should be secured on all positions, not only from the people conducting the analysis, but also from individual employees and their supervisors.[1]

The advantages of a position-classification plan have been discussed repeatedly in library literature.[2] It is a tool for recruitment, placement, promotion, and transfer of personnel. It is invaluable in training and in evaluating efficiency. It is a basis for an equitable compensation plan. In giving a detailed picture of each position, its relationship to other positions and to the whole, the plan presents a clearer understanding of the organization of the library. It serves administration in general by revealing organizational defects, thus, pointing the way to realignment of positions and more efficient planning and budgeting. Finally, being an impartial, systematic approach, it avoids purely personalized treatment of work and pay problems and, therefore, becomes a positive step in the improvement of staff morale.

The whole process of gathering information, analyzing and classifying jobs,

---

[1] The ideas in this paragraph were taken from Herman G. Pope, "Classification of Positions," in Chicago, University, Graduate Library School, Library Institute, *Personnel Administration in Libraries*; papers presented before the Library Institute at the University of Chicago, August 27-September 1, 1945, edited with an introduction by Lowell Martin (Chicago: Univ. of Chicago Pr., c1946), p.36-37.

[2] See especially the references by Eleanor Hitt and Ralph D. Remley, listed in the SELECTED BIBLIOGRAPHY, which emphasize the advantages of position classification.

and constructing a position-classification plan is referred to in this manual as a position-classification survey. The persons who conduct the survey are termed analysts.

Job Analysis

Preliminary to the establishment of a classification plan, each position must be analyzed in terms of its duties and its relationship to other positions. Job analysis has been defined as "the process of determining, by observation and study, and reporting pertinent information relating to the nature of a specific job. It is the determination of the tasks which comprise the job and of the skills, knowledges, abilities, and responsibilities required of the worker for successful performance and which differentiate the job from all others."[3] The basis for this analysis is a written record of each task performed within the position, together with the amount or percentage of time spent on each, and the type and amount of supervision given or received.

Time Study

When daily work sheets are kept by employees, recording each task performed during the day with the amount of time spent on each, the resulting statistics on the tasks and the time consumed by them constitute a time study.

Job Description

The assembled information concerning the duties and responsibilities of the job, when rewritten for purposes of uniformity and clarity, is termed a job description.

Job Specification

When a statement is added to the job description, listing the requirements sought in the individual for a particular job, it becomes a job specification.

Position

The term, position,[4] is used to mean all duties and responsibilities assigned to one individual, but it must be strictly disassociated from that individual. Therefore, it is necessary to emphasize continually that it is the position which is analyzed and classified, not the performance, ability, or characteristics of the person occupying it. Education, experience, skills, and personal traits are factors in the classification of positions, but they are expressed in terms of the minimum qualifications required of an individual upon original entrance to a given position, and have no connection with the qualifications which the present incumbent happens to possess or lack. This

---

[3] U.S. Bureau of Manpower Utilization, Occupational Analysis and Manning Tables Division, Training and Reference Manual for Job Analysis (Washington: War Manpower Commission, 1944), p.1.

[4] In this manual the terms, position and job, are used interchangeably.

does not imply that the person cannot influence the development of the position, but it does mean that the concept of the position must be in terms of the work rather than of the person who does the work. In fact, the position may even be vacant, but its duties can still be analyzed.

In analyzing a given position, its duties must be recorded as they currently exist, not as they existed in the past, nor as they should exist. If duties are shifted or major changes are made in a position after the analysis, then a reanalysis will be necessary, based on the position as it exists at that time.

Classes of Positions

The process of classification consists of grouping positions into classes according to the degree of difficulty and responsibility involved. This implies that in these respects each position in a class will be similar to all other positions in that class. A class of positions will consist of all positions, irrespective of their location, that are sufficiently alike in duties and responsibilities to be given the same descriptive title, to require substantially the same qualifications, and to be accorded the same rate of pay.

Class Title

Each class of positions is given a descriptive name or a title which differentiates it from all other classes.

Class Definition

The class to which positions have been allocated is defined by a written statement describing those duties and responsibilities of the positions within the class which differentiate it from all other classes.

Class Specification

The class specification is composed of: (1) the class title; (2) the class definition; (3) examples of typical tasks; and (4) the minimum qualifications necessary to perform the work of the class.

Classification Grades

After positions are grouped into classes, the latter may be grouped according to level into grades. All classes in the same grade will be substantially equal in respect to difficulty and responsibility, though they vary greatly in character, subject matter, or function. They must require the same basic qualifications and call for the same rate of pay.

Services

Classification grades may further be grouped into services, although such grouping is not essential and is made for convenience only. This grouping is made on broad lines according to the general character of the duties. Thus, the professional positions fall into one service, the clerical into another, and the custodial into a third.

Salary Schedule

Positions may be analyzed and classified without regard to salaries, but the usual culmination of a classification survey is a revision of the rates of pay, and often a reexamination of pay practices and policies.

The commonly accepted principle that equal work should call for equal pay naturally implies that more difficult and responsible work calls for higher pay and less difficult and less responsible work for lower pay. A salary schedule is a series of salary ranges assigned to the classes in the position-classification plan, governed by the difficulty and responsibility of the positions within each class. It is customary to have a range rather than one salary rate for each class, this range consisting of a minimum and maximum rate with several intermediate steps.

Salary Increments

The intermediate steps on the salary range between the minimum and maximum of the class provide salary increases for the individual as he advances from the minimum because of increased experience and efficiency.

Chapter II

PRELIMINARY PLANNING

Presenting the Idea to Those Concerned

A number of preliminary steps are necessary before a position-classification survey is begun, the first being a careful presentation of the idea to all concerned with the survey.

The initiative for setting up such a study may come from any one of several sources: from the board, the administrator, the personnel department, or the employees of the library; but in all cases, the decision to develop a classification plan is subject to the approval of the governing body. In presenting the proposal, it should be emphasized that the chief goal of such a plan is to analyze each position in the library completely, objectively, and accurately, so that all positions may be classified in an equitable relationship to one another.

It is vital to the success of any position-classification survey that a definite understanding be reached with the governing body as to the effects of the installation of the resulting classification upon the individual employee. Fears in regard to reduced salaries or lowered rank will inevitably arise. It is strongly advised that assurance be given by the administration that no salaries will be cut as a result of the classification and that present ranking will be maintained if at all possible.[1] Many misunderstandings can be avoided if every effort is made to explain the purpose of position classification. It should be stressed at every available opportunity that it is the JOB which is being analyzed, not the INDIVIDUAL, and that the survey is not to be regarded in any way as an investigation of the performance of the employee on the job. It should also be emphasized that the full benefits of the plan are not always apparent at the time of installation, but that they often increase over extended periods.

Selecting the Agency to Do the Work

The success of a position-classification survey depends greatly upon the wise selection of an agency to carry it forward. Outside agencies, existing personnel departments, or employee committees may be considered as the most effective vehicles, depending upon individual circumstances. A combination of these agencies might also be used. There may even be an advantage in having a joint employee and board committee work on the project.

Outside agencies -- There are a few excellent private agencies[2] which make

---

[1] The status of employees in libraries operating under civil service will, of course, be governed by local regulations in regard to classification and rank.
[2] The A.L.A. Board on Personnel Administration can refer librarians to reputable firms qualified to do a position-classification survey. This board can also give advice in the planning of a survey.

a business of conducting position analyses and establishing position-classification plans. If at all possible, such a firm or individual should be employed, if not to conduct the entire survey, at least to render advisory services. Such service can also be obtained from civil service or central personnel agencies of the city or the state. Every library should explore the possibility of obtaining some assistance before attempting a self-survey without help or guidance. Charges made by private agencies are not prohibitive.[3] It is even possible for several small libraries within a limited geographical area to conduct surveys at the same time, employing one agency and sharing the cost. If there seems to be no justification for paying outside help when the library staff can give the service free, it should first be carefully considered just how much of this service would really be "free." Salary costs for staff members doing work, which requires far more time and study for them than it would for an expert in the field, will be real, even though they are hidden. The practice of employees donating their own time to the survey cannot be condoned as good personnel practice. Library service might even suffer while these staff members are taken from their regular duties to study for and carry out the survey. When a committee is assigned to such a project only part time, the period of completion is prolonged and some positions may undergo changes, thus, requiring rechecking. The administration should carefully study all of these hidden costs before deciding not to employ outside help.

Personnel departments -- An increasing number of large libraries have created personnel departments, and such departments often exist in large industrial organizations where special libraries are located. Representatives of these departments should certainly be active in a classification survey. In fact, they should assume leadership in initiating and carrying out such a program, but since such departments often consist of only one or two professional members, outside help will usually be needed.

Employee committees -- If the decision is made to utilize staff members to conduct or assist with the survey, extreme care should be taken to select individuals who have a reputation for impartiality among the employees. They must also be willing to spend considerable time in learning the procedures and methods employed in position classification. The committee should also represent as many phases of the work of the library as possible. It should include both professional and nonprofessional workers, staff members with long service records, and those new enough to the system to present a fresh viewpoint.

An employee committee may be used even though an outside agency is to be employed. Under the guidance of such an agency, it can do much of the preliminary work and be an important link between the agency, the staff, and the administration. It may be useful in an advisory capacity or in the studying and reporting on special problems.

Qualifications of the analysts -- In whatever manner the analysts are selected, they should possess certain skills and qualities. The good analyst

---

[3] One firm has done a survey in a small library in one day at a cost of $60. A survey job for a larger library was done by mail for $300. These figures are not quoted as rates but merely as some indication of what is meant by "not prohibitive."

will, of course, have a knowledge of the theory and technique of job analysis and position classification, or have the ability to acquire that knowledge. He will combine an agreeable personality with understanding, tact, and patience. He will get along well with people and be able to see various viewpoints. He must be so fair that all will recognize that fairness. Moreover, he must be able to acquire knowledge of the organization and functions of each department and of the objectives and methods of the entire system. It is necessary for him to be able to get at the facts, weigh their relative importance, combine and classify the material concisely and accurately, and put the findings clearly into writing.

Number of analysts needed -- The size of the survey staff depends primarily on the number of positions to be classified. Because it is necessary to analyze positions as they exist, it is advisable to complete the survey as quickly as possible and, therefore, in a large library a sizeable survey staff is required.[4] Even in a very small library it is well to have at least two persons on the survey staff in order that more than one opinion will be available for decisions in questionable cases.

Deciding What Positions Are to Be Included in the Survey

The scope of the position-classification survey should be clearly defined at the outset by determining the positions to be covered. In some cases, this will be decided by legal provisions. If there are no such restrictions, it is advisable to include all positions (professional, nonprofessional, janitorial, part-time and full-time) in the survey.[5] In this way, the most complete, detailed, and accurate picture of the work of the library can be obtained.

Selecting the Method

The next step in planning is the selection of the method to be used in conducting the survey. Such considerations as time, cost, and number of positions to be surveyed will influence the decision.

There are four principal methods of obtaining information about the duties and responsibilities of positions: (1) questionnaires; (2) interviews with employees and supervisors; (3) direct observation; and (4) a combination of these three.

The questionnaire -- In using this method, each employee fills out a questionnaire form pertaining to his own job. Its great advantage lies in the fact that the employee is the best source of information concerning the duties and responsibilities of his particular job. At the same time, he becomes an active participant in the survey. A drawback to using this method alone is that the

---

[4] Possibly one analyst for every group of twenty positions is sufficient. In the largest libraries probably more should be included in each group so that the survey staff itself will not be too large.

[5] In a university or school library where a great number of students are employed by the hour, these positions might be included in the survey only by types of jobs performed rather than by individual positions.

individual is frequently unable to describe his work adequately. He may overrate or underrate it, which results in a distorted evaluation. This disadvantage may be offset somewhat by asking for a brief statement from the supervisor[6] concerning each job under his supervision. It is necessary to accompany the questionnaire with adequate oral and written instructions.

The interview -- If the interview method is used, the information about the job is acquired in an interview between the analyst and the employee supplemented by a checking interview with the supervisor. The disadvantage of using this system alone lies in the fact that important points may be omitted or forgotten even though notes of these interviews are kept for future study. When skillfully executed, the interview is an effective follow-up to the written questionnaire, as it often brings to light additional information about positions, inadvertently or purposely omitted from the employee's questionnaire.

Direct observation -- Frequently it will be necessary for the analyst actually to observe the work being done in a position in order to clarify the picture of the job. Obviously, it would be time-consuming to conduct the entire survey by such a method, but it is a valuable technique when combined with others.

Combination of the three methods -- A combination of the three methods mentioned above is recommended. It results in a well-rounded picture of positions and brings together the points of view, both written and oral, of the employee and his immediate supervisor. In case of disagreement or confusion, the observation of the analyst enters the picture. The interviews which follow the written questionnaire afford an opportunity for the analyst, the supervisor, and the employee to reach an agreement on the description of each position.

Assembling and Studying the Necessary Tools

The final step before actually beginning the survey is the assembling and study of the survey tools. These will undoubtedly vary in different organizations, but certain basic ones will be common to all groups. Most important of these are pay-roll rosters, budget documents, organization charts, legal provisions, and staff and departmental manuals.

Pay-roll rosters provide a complete up-to-date list of employees. From them it can be determined how many questionnaires are necessary for each unit. These rosters are also useful for checking in questionnaires when they are returned, and to note changes in personnel during the course of the survey. Budget documents may list the number and kinds of positions in the various departments. Organization charts reveal the relationship among positions and provide a basis for clearer understanding of the operations of the library. If it is found that these charts do not present an accurate and current picture, they should be redrawn by the analysts. The analysts must acquaint themselves

---

[6] In this manual the term, supervisor, is used to refer to any person who is responsible for overseeing the work of others. In a small library it would probably be the chief librarian. In a larger library it might be a department or division chief or even an assistant.

with any legal provisions which might affect the development or administration of the position-classification plan. Charter provisions, ordinances, certification laws, etc. should be examined to determine their bearing, if any, on position classification. Where civil service or personnel rules exist, they should be reviewed. Departmental and staff manuals of routines and procedures and reports of activities should be read for the light they throw on work processes and problems. The study of these survey tools provides the analysts with some basic knowledge of the work of the positions to be analyzed and classified.

Unless previously experienced in this type of work, the analysts should read and study some of the basic books on the subject of position classification. Even though most of these books are designed for government, industry, or business, they will be of great help to the analysts as the theory and techniques apply equally to library work. (See SELECTED BIBLIOGRAPHY, p. 61-62.)

If an employee committee has been selected to do a portion of the survey under the guidance of a professional agency, the point at which the agency actually enters the survey might be delayed until after the questionnaires have been returned (see p. 13) or after the job specifications have been written (see p. 16-17).

Chapter III

CONDUCTING THE JOB ANALYSIS

After the preliminary planning has been completed, the persons selected to conduct the position-classification survey are ready to begin the analysis of positions. "Basically, there are but three parts to the analysis of any job: (1) the job must be completely and accurately identified; (2) the tasks of the job must be completely and accurately described; (3) the requirements the job makes upon the worker for successful performance must be indicated."[1] The second of these three parts which describes the tasks or duties is extremely important, since the ultimate classification of the position depends upon the exact nature, scope, and difficulty of the tasks involved.

Preparing the Job Analysis Questionnaire

The questionnaire is one of the principal tools used in acquiring the information on each job to be analyzed. Therefore, the preparation of this form should be given careful consideration.

A job analysis questionnaire contains a series of questions designed to draw out the essential information concerning the position. The following points must be considered: (1) what identifying data are to be included; (2) who is to fill it out; (3) what general form of expression is to be used in listing the tasks; (4) what method is to be employed in determining the amount of time spent on individual tasks; and (5) how supervision is to be indicated. (See JOB ANALYSIS QUESTIONNAIRE, p. 63-64.)

Identifying data -- The questionnaire should provide space to indicate for a given position: (1) the name of the incumbent; (2) department or branch; (3) position title; (4) total hours of work; (5) daily schedule; and (6) rate of pay.

Who fills out the form -- Because the best source of information concerning a job is the employee doing the work, he must fill out the basic part of the questionnaire describing his duties. As a check for accuracy, the supervisor should be given opportunity to amplify or comment on this description and to add his own statements regarding what he considers the essential characteristics of the position. Only if a position is vacant should the supervisor fill out the entire questionnaire.

How the tasks are listed and described -- Adequate space should be provided on the form for listing all duties which are contained in a given job. The regular duties are usually listed first and those performed occasionally or periodically, and so designated, are listed next. Certain uniformity of statements may be agreed upon at the outset. For example, such phrases as "Assisting patrons in the use of the card catalog," "Sorting and filing book cards,"

---

[1] U.S. Bureau of Manpower Utilization, Occupational Analysis and Manning Tables Division, <u>Training and Reference Manual for Job Analysis</u> (Washington: War Manpower Commission, 1944), p.1.

and "Registering borrowers" will appear in many positions. If they are in uniform terminology, they are more easily checked by the analyst. The A.L.A. list of duties performed in libraries[2] will prove useful to the analyst as a guide for terminology, but such a listing should not be given the employee for it may put words into his mouth, thus, defeating the purpose of the questionnaire, which is to get a firsthand description of his duties.

The time spent on tasks -- The amount of time required to perform each task or duty of the job should be a part of the questionnaire, and this information may be secured by a time study. A record of tasks is kept regularly for several days or weeks with the exact amount of time spent on each. A typical period of time should be chosen for the study, which includes all normal duties of the job. Daily work sheets are kept and, at the end of the period of time chosen, a summary of the tasks is transferred to the job analysis questionnaire, including the time spent on each task. Since the length of time required to conduct a reliable time study is an important item to be considered, and since no period of time is absolutely typical, another method can be used. It is possible to estimate the percentage of time spent on tasks without benefit of the time study, or the employee may indicate his time as so many hours per day on a particular task, and, in the case of tasks which are periodic, so many hours per week, month, or year. If a time study is made, the work sheets, after transference of the material to the questionnaire, are no longer needed in the job analysis, but they do comprise a by-product which may be utilized in reorganization of work or routines. (See DAILY WORK SHEETS, p. 65-66.)

Indication of supervision -- The questions on the form which bring out the relationships of each position in the organization are important. Space should be provided for indicating the supervision over others and the extent of supervision received in the position. This may be done by a series of questions concerning the nature and degree of supervision.

Preparing Instructions for Employees

Written instructions are usually prepared to accompany the questionnaire and are primarily designed to give detailed information on how to fill out each item. Suggestions should be given in respect to the form and content of describing the tasks, including examples of what are and what are not adequate phrases. For instance "filing cards" is not as adequate as "filing catalog cards" or "filing registration cards." It should be emphasized that the description of the job is to be the employee's own statement and is not to be altered in any manner by supervisor or analyst, although it may be changed by agreement during the interview. A time limit should be indicated for the return of the questionnaires, probably five days to a week, and instructions given as to how they are to be routed. Signatures should be required of the employee and of all supervisors of the employee, and a time limit of not more than one week imposed on supervisors. (See SAMPLE INSTRUCTIONS, p. 67-69.)

---
[2]American Library Association, Board on Personnel Administration, Subcommittee on Analysis of Library Duties, Descriptive List of Professional and Nonprofessional Duties in Libraries (Preliminary draft; Chicago: American Library Assn., 1948)

Making Arrangements with Supervisors

Before distributing the questionnaires to the employees, details should be presented and explained to the supervisors. Whenever possible, the timing of the analysis should be adjusted to their satisfaction. This is particularly true in the event that a time study is made as a part of the analysis. The supervisors can best choose the most typical time for the study in their own departments and the time which will least interfere with departmental operations. They can also give advice as to the proper length of time to run such a study, whether a true picture of the jobs can be obtained in a few days, or whether it will take two weeks or longer. They should be instructed not to change the duties of any position, insofar as possible, while the survey is being done.

It is advisable to impress upon the supervisors the fact that each employee, after receiving adequate instructions, is expected to work on his questionnaire without suggestions or supervision from any source. They should also be instructed not to allow employees to collaborate when filling out the questionnaires.

Explaining the Survey Plans to Employees

One of the most vital and continuing steps in the development of the position-classification survey is that of explaining the plan to employees. The paragraph headed, Preparing Instructions for Employees (p. 11), explains how written material should be prepared for distribution with the questionnaire. Before it is distributed, however, it is advisable to explain the plan by means of house organs or bulletins, group meetings, and individual contact. As a general rule, all these methods should be utilized, but obviously the smaller the library, the less need for more formal ways of presentation. Group meetings, whether the staff be large or small, are particularly useful for the opportunity they afford for discussion and questions.

The purposes of these frequent and detailed explanations are: (1) to present the objectives and methods of the survey to all affected by it; (2) to clear up possible misunderstanding, suspicion, and apprehension on the part of the employee as to the possible effect of the survey upon him personally; (3) to emphasize the fact that it is the duties and responsibilities attached to the _position_ which are being studied and not the ability of the _person_ doing the work; (4) to impress upon the employee the value of a full and complete statement of duties which he prepares independently; (5) to inform employees of the identity of the analysts designated to conduct the survey; and (6) to make it clear that the analysts will be available for consultation and assistance. If these points are thoroughly understood at the outset, the cooperation and support of all employees will be obtained more easily.

In addition to the initial presentation of the plan, it is essential to keep the employees informed of the progress of the survey. Each new step should be preceded by news of what is to take place. Explaining what is being done at all times inspires confidence and helps to assure continued cooperation. Never, during the whole process of setting up a position-classification scheme, should the necessity for the disseminating of information be forgotten.

Distributing and Returning the Questionnaires

As soon as the plan has been explained to the entire staff, the questionnaires and instructions are distributed. A careful check must be kept to make certain that each employee receives the material. It is desirable to have the questionnaires filled out in duplicate, one for the employee to retain and one to be returned to the analysts. It may even be desirable to fill out the forms in triplicate, the third copy being used by the analyst for filing purposes. The time limit for the return of the questionnaires and the prearranged system of routing should be strictly observed so that all completed forms reach the analyst at a definite time.

At the time of distribution of the material, analysts should be assigned to groups of employees and should be easily available to the employees for consultation during the process of filling out the questionnaires. Their first job is to see that every employee understands the instructions. It is also expedient to have the analysts conduct the subsequent interviews and follow through the complete analysis with the group originally assigned to them.

As the questionnaires are completed and returned, each should be carefully checked and any missing ones traced. Those which have been filled out inadequately or incorrectly can be noted and corrected at the time of the interviews, unless they are so badly done that it would seem advisable for the employee to correct them immediately. (See COMPLETED JOB ANALYSIS QUESTIONNAIRES, p. 70-75.)

Arranging and Studying Questionnaires

To facilitate study of the questionnaires, they are arranged according to main departmental units, the questionnaires of all employees under the same supervisor falling together. If the forms are filled out in triplicate, one set may remain in this arrangement, the other being used as a working copy. This first sorting and study of the questionnaire give the analyst an over-all view of the unit assigned to him. More careful and complete study is made in subsequent steps of the analysis.

Writing Job Descriptions[3]

After the questionnaires are completed and arranged, the analyst writes a job description for each position assigned to him. The job description consists of: (1) the job title; (2) the job summary; and (3) the work performed. (See SAMPLE JOB DESCRIPTIONS, p. 76-78.)

The job title -- At this point in the analysis, the present position title is used for the job title. This should be changed on the job description at a

---

[3]It is possible to omit the step, Writing Job Descriptions, if the questionnaires have been correctly filled out and enough uniformity of terminology exists for adequate comparison of questionnaires. In the small library where only one position will probably be allocated to a class, this step may very easily be dropped.

later time if a more adequate title is assigned to the position.

The job summary -- This is a sketch of the job as a whole, not the details of the job and should indicate the source of supervision.

The work performed -- The most important part of the job description is the section describing the work performed on the job. It is a listing of the various tasks, taken from the questionnaire and rewritten for uniform terminology, with the amount or percentage of time spent on each.

The important details of the job should be explained so logically, concisely, and specifically, that a totally uninformed reader can obtain a clear concept of the work performed. This means that it is usually necessary to rephrase the employee's words, either amplifying the statements or more often restating them in briefer form. Sufficient detail should be given to show an accurate picture of the job, but only pertinent details should be recorded. It should be kept in mind that the description is not a manual on how to do the job. Well chosen words with specific meanings should be employed and uniformity of phrasing is desirable. If the description is properly phrased to show the difficult and responsible nature of the duties, the use of adjectives is unnecessary and should be avoided. Each sentence might begin with a functional verb, the participle form being convenient and satisfactory[4] (i.e., "Filing catalog cards," "Writing overdues").

It may be necessary for the sake of clarity and conciseness to group individual tasks. If percentages of time are used, they must also be grouped, and a check made to see that the total approximates 100%. When rephrasing to standard terminology and regrouping for clarity, no change should be made in the meaning of the original statements. It is advisable to attach the job description to the corresponding job analysis questionnaire so that all information concerning the job, up to this point, is together.

Conducting Interviews

After studying the questionnaires and writing tentative job descriptions, the analyst is ready to interview the individual employee. This, it will be recalled, is the second step of the combined method which was recommended for an accurate and complete job analysis. The purpose of the interview is to verify the job description the analyst has written and to secure additional information which might have been omitted on the questionnaire. The analyst will also wish to question the employee on how much of the work has been completed before it reaches him, what his responsibilities are in regard to the work, and what responsibilities for it belong to the supervisor.

Example:

In the JOB ANALYSIS QUESTIONNAIRE of the desk assistant (see p. 70-71), several items need interpretation before a final job description is written.

---
[4] See American Library Association, Board on Personnel Administration, Subcommittee on Analysis of Library Duties, op. cit., as a guide.

1. The item, "Charging, taking in, and slipping books, registering borrowers, helping patrons to find books," obviously contains a number of different elements. They were grouped because these operations are all done during a continuous loan desk assignment. Further investigation reveals that "Helping patrons to find books" means the location and selection of books. Since this is a professional task[5] and the other items in this group are nonprofessional, the percentage of 50% for all is broken down to 40% and 10% in the SAMPLE JOB DESCRIPTION (see p. 76).

2. Questions concerning the item, "Setting up displays," reveal that the employee has also planned the displays, thus, adding a professional element to this task.

3. "Book talks" were found to be book reviews and talks on reading, planned in this position and given to such groups as the P.T.A. and womens' study groups.

There are certain fundamental techniques in interviewing which should be followed. Some of the accepted rules are:

1. Arrange for the interview beforehand with both the employee and his immediate supervisor.
2. Provide for privacy.
3. Be sure the employee understands the purpose of the interview and knows who is to interview him.
4. Be courteous enough to address the employee by name.
5. Be thoroughly familiar with the job under discussion so that you can ask intelligent and direct questions.
6. Avoid implying the answer to your own questions.
7. Encourage the employee to express himself freely, but do not let him wander from the question under consideration.
8. Show interest in the information received.
9. Close the interview promptly when the necessary information has been acquired.
10. Express appreciation to the employee for his assistance.
11. Write up your notes on the interview immediately.[6]

During the interview, the analyst, through diplomacy and tact, must enlist the employee's interest and awaken in him a desire to furnish a true picture of his work. He should be made to feel that he is the expert concerning his own job, and this is his opportunity to clarify the information given on the questionnaire. The interviewer, however, must use judgment in interpreting the information given, since there is a natural tendency for some employees to lay undue stress upon the importance of their own duties, and for others to

---

[5]The authority for terming these tasks professional or nonprofessional is American Library Association, Board on Personnel Administration, Subcommittee on Analysis of Library Duties, op. cit.
[6]For more detailed information on interviewing techniques see Walter V. Bingham and B. V. Moore, How to Interview (3d rev. ed.; N.Y.: Harper, 1941)

minimize their importance. This may not be done consciously, but, because the employee has such intimate knowledge of his own job, a true sense of proportion is lost.

Accuracy of the tentative job description should be further checked by an interview with the supervisor. The employee's idea of his job and the supervisor's idea of it are not always the same; furthermore, the latter's opinion is not necessarily correct. The analyst must harmonize these different points of view, and he may find it necessary actually to observe the employee at his work to gain a clearer understanding which will help him resolve these differences. Thus, the third technique of the combined method for conducting a job analysis comes into play. Job descriptions should not be considered final until analyst, employee, and supervisor agree that the description as written is a complete, fair, and accurate picture of the job. This may mean several revisions before one acceptable to all is written.

Writing Job Specifications

During the interview, the employee is asked what qualifications he considers necessary for his job. An opinion should also be sought from the supervisor concerning qualifications for all positions under his supervision. Here again the analyst may find conflicting views. Employees may think that the qualifications they possess are adequate, or even higher than necessary, for their jobs. Supervisors may favor standards which are too high or may have a prejudice for or against a particular kind of training. In order to resolve these opinions, the analyst must understand the service requirements of the library and possess a working knowledge of personnel standards in other fields. He may also wish to consult other people who are familiar with the type of work in question. He must not allow the qualifications to be set too rigidly or too high for the duties performed and the compensation received, nor be unduly influenced by the qualifications of the incumbent.

Once the differences of opinion are resolved, a statement is added to the job description listing the qualifications. These are usually expressed as the minimum standards of education, training, experience, skills, knowledge, abilities, and personality requirements needed. "Desirable" qualifications may be given, but "minimum" qualifications are used in the A.L.A. classification and pay plans.[7]

When the qualification statement is added to the job description, it becomes a job specification.[8] This step completes the job analysis part of the survey,

---

[7] American Library Association, Board on Personnel Administration, Classification and Pay Plans for Municipal Public Libraries (Chicago: American Library Assn., 1939)

American Library Association, Board on Personnel Administration, Subcommittee on Budgets, Compensation and Schemes of Service for Libraries Connected with Universities, Colleges and Teacher Training Institutions, Classification and Pay Plans for Libraries in Institutions of Higher Education (2d ed.; Chicago: American Library Assn., 1947), 3v.

[8] If the step concerning the writing of a job description is omitted (see footnote 3, p. 13) a qualification statement should be attached to the original questionnaire.

and the analysts are ready to begin classifying the positions.

Example:

To prepare a job specification for the junior reference librarian position, add the following to the SAMPLE JOB DESCRIPTION (see p. 78):

Minimum qualifications

1. Education
    a. Graduation from an accredited college or university
    b. Graduation from an accredited library school
2. Experience
    a. None required, though desirable
3. Skills, abilities, etc.
    a. Knowledge of reference methods and practices
    b. Acquaintance with reference tools
    c. Understanding of library organization, procedures, policy, aims, and service
4. Personal
    a. Initiative
    b. Resourcefulness
    c. Accuracy
    d. Perseverance
    e. Good memory
    f. Ability to meet the public well

Chapter IV

FACTORS TO BE CONSIDERED IN CLASSIFYING POSITIONS

The next step in the developing of a position-classification plan is to establish classes to which all positions will eventually be assigned. Before this can be done, however, careful study must be given to the factors which will govern the setting up of classes and the grading of individual positions for logical placement in these classes.

The factors in position classification fall into four broad areas: (1) difficulty and complexity of duties; (2) nonsupervisory responsibilities; (3) supervisory and administrative responsibilities; and (4) qualification standards.[1] These factors are the guide posts which enable the analyst to determine that certain positions are sufficiently similar to be grouped in the same class. They will be discussed in detail in this chapter.

Difficulty and Complexity of Duties

As used in this respect, "difficulty" of a task does not refer to the ease or difficulty which any employee experiences in performing it, but rather it is the ranking of duties as to their difficulty and complexity, irrespective of the person performing them. The principal elements to be determined are: (1) how far the work has progressed when presented to the employee; (2) how the work is assigned; (3) procedure followed by the employee; (4) relationship of one employee's work to others; and (5) variety and scope of duties.

How far work has progressed -- A complete picture of a position cannot always be obtained by confining attention to its particular tasks. Reference must also be made to other positions that involve work upon this same task both before and after it reaches the position in question. This involves a study of the flow of work from inception to completion, showing how and by whom each operation is performed.

Examples:

(1) A clerk is responsible for all overdue routines, removing cards from circulation files, checking shelves, looking up names and addresses, and typing notices. In this case, the assignment is carried out by the employee from its beginning to its end. If the clerk does nothing but type the overdue notices, he is responsible for only the final step in the flow of work, all other steps having been completed before the assignment reaches him.

---

[1] These are the factors used in Civil Service Assembly of the United States and Canada, Committee on Position-classification and Pay Plans in the Public Service, *Position-classification in the Public Service* (Chicago: The Assembly, 1941), p. 91-131, and this material has been drawn upon heavily for this chapter of the manual.

(2) A catalog librarian uses Library of Congress cards, and, therefore, a great deal of descriptive cataloging, subject heading, and classifying has been done before the work reaches his position. On the other hand, he may do a great deal of original cataloging, making all decisions in the position.

How work is assigned -- In order to determine the level of responsibility for any position, it is necessary to determine the basis on which assignments are made. In some departments, assignments may be made without discrimination as to their difficulty and complexity. Over a period of time, each employee has a mixture of work representing various degrees of difficulty. In such cases, the aggregate difficulty of the duties of each position is the same. On the other hand, a supervisor may examine all tasks, determine their relative difficulty, segregate them into several groups, and make the assignments accordingly. The degree of difficulty of duties then varies in these different groups.

Examples:

(1) In a reference department, the employees may take all questions in turn - informational, research, etc. The research questions, however, may be segregated and given to one or more employees while the simpler types of questions are assigned to others.

(2) In a catalog department, the foreign books may be separated from the English books and assigned to different individuals.

(3) In a catalog department, the simple and more difficult card typing may be separated and assigned to different individuals.

Procedure followed by the employee -- The work done by the employee himself must be considered in terms of the procedure he follows, the plans or actions he initiates, and the decisions he makes. A study of the work done should reveal the mental processes or the manual operations involved. The degree of difficulty can be evaluated to some extent by a consideration of the qualifications necessary to the performance of the work.

Example:

A clerk may do filing and typing in a catalog department. It is necessary to know what *kind* of filing and what *kind* of typing he is doing. The files may be relatively simple numerical or alphabetical ones, or they may be more complicated subject files. The typing may be from well prepared copy, or it may require some interpretation or arrangement on the part of the typist.

Relationship of one employee's work to others -- In tracing the flow of work, it is apparent that few positions are isolated entities, most of them being definitely connected with one another. They are interdependent in their action and combine to form the whole process necessary to the completed work. Thus, in appraising the difficulty of the work in an individual position, it is necessary to analyze the kind and degree of supervision exercised over it and to consider its duties and responsibilities in respect to other positions having work closely related to it.

Examples:

(1) A clerk at the circulation desk is responsible for such simple routine duties as charging and discharging books, filing book cards, and shelving books, but an immediate supervisor is always near to be consulted or to take over if deviation from the routine is necessary. In case deviation from set policies or exceptions to rules are indicated, a still higher authority may need to be consulted.

(2) A branch librarian may be charged with the responsibility for a neighborhood activity. The supervisor may give advice and final approval of the plans, but the branch librarian is fully responsible for carrying out the project.

Variety and scope of duties -- The variety and scope of duties in various positions may differ greatly. Some positions involve one duty or one closely connected series of duties, while another may be made up of many relatively unconnected tasks. It might at first appear that this variety of tasks would add to its difficulty of accomplishment and call for an equal variety of qualifications. The performance of a number of simple duties, however, may be no more difficult nor require more in the way of qualifications than one duty. Variety becomes significant only when the level of difficulty of the various tasks advances and a broader scope of knowledge and ability is required.

Examples:

(1) A clerk who charges and discharges books, files cards, and shelves books has a variety of tasks, but they are on relatively the same level.

(2) The clerk who does all the above tasks but also has the responsibility of waiting on the public, answering questions, and helping the patron find books has added duties on a higher level than the above mentioned.

(3) The librarian who spends his time cataloging books, answering reference questions, and acting as readers' advisor must have a broader scope of knowledge than the person engaged in any one of these tasks on a full-time basis, providing that the level of difficulty is approximately the same.

Nonsupervisory Responsibilities

Every position has responsibility of some kind and degree vested in it. Certain responsibilities, such as the common traits of integrity, honesty, and industry, so obviously apply to all positions that they are not considered classification factors. The principal nonsupervisory responsibilities can be reduced to the following categories: (1) independence of action or decision; (2) recommending plans or policies; (3) money, supplies, equipment; (4) accuracy; and (5) public contacts.

Independence of action and decision — Independence of action or decision is indicative in some measure of the level of responsibility in a given position. It may further denote freedom from prescribed work methods and routine techniques and involve some initiative and a degree of authority for finality of action. As work increases in difficulty and scope, this type of responsibility also increases. Because responsibilities are relative, and the various positions in the organization are interdependent, it is frequently necessary to trace the whole course of responsibility for a certain type of work from its beginning to its end, in order to determine the degree of responsibility vested in each position.

In appraising the independence of action and decision, it is also necessary to trace the lines of control from above and to determine the degree of supervision exercised. Work reaching a given position with its techniques established and its decisions made, or work which is carefully reviewed upon completion, entails less responsibility than work which has little supervisory direction. Thus, in general, control or supervision from above reduces the independence of action or decision in that position.

Examples:

(1) In the example cited under the item, Relationship of one employee's work to others (see p. 20), the clerk at the circulation desk has little independence of action or decision. His immediate supervisor has more, and the higher supervisory authority exercises far more than either. If the question involves library or board general policies, the matter would have to be taken to the highest authority. Thus, the responsibility for circulation routines can be traced from the lowest to the highest position concerned with it.

(2) The typist in the catalog department has all of her cards revised so has no independence of action or decision. On the other hand, a clerk may file all registration cards without revision and, thus, has full responsibility for the correctness of that file.

Responsibility for recommending plans and policies — Positions may occasionally be found, especially in larger libraries, which have little responsibility for supervision of other employees, but do involve responsibility for developing policies, plans, and programs. They may be "staff" as opposed to "line" positions.[2] Their evaluation depends upon the scope, importance, and difficulty of the problems involved. It is also necessary to know the condition of the work at the start and the extent of supervision and review over decisions made.

Example:

Elements of this nonsupervisory responsibility are present in such positions as an adult education advisor, a personnel officer, a public relations director, and an administrative or research assistant in a large

---

[2] See Clara W. Herbert, Personnel Administration in Public Libraries; with a chapter by Althea H. Warren and Lora A. Roden (Chicago: American Library Assn., 1939), p.7-11.

library. Insofar as these positions deal with the recommending of plans and policies, of methods and work flow, they have this nonsupervisory responsibility with little or no responsibility for actual work supervision.

Responsibility for money, supplies, equipment -- These responsibilities may sometimes be overemphasized in connection with a given position (which is probably a reflection of the importance they assume in personal affairs). In evaluating them, the degree of responsibility is dependent upon the controls which govern them. Thus, in order that the responsibility be of sufficient weight to warrant consideration in classification, a real responsibility for the care of things of special value should coexist with reasonable freedom from close supervision.

Examples:

The employee who takes in fine money at a circulation desk and keeps an account of that money has a slight degree of this responsibility. The order librarian, who handles large sums of money for the purchase of books without close or frequent check, has this nonsupervisory responsibility in a fairly large degree. The supply manager, who selects and orders furniture and equipment, paper stock, etc., carries this nonsupervisory responsibility to a great extent.

Responsibility for accuracy -- A need for accuracy is present in nearly all positions in the library. In most cases, it is a factor to be considered in connection with the employee's efficiency of performance and in this sense is not a classification factor. It is necessary, therefore, to determine whether accuracy is a factor of carefulness or one of advanced qualifications, and whether it is required to such a degree as to be difficult of attainment for the employee of normal training. The potential consequence of errors must also be considered.

Examples:

(1) Accuracy as a factor is present in the position of the reference librarian who has ultimate responsibility for giving correct information, the catalog librarian who makes the final check on the correctness of catalog information, and the clerk who orders Library of Congress cards without revision. Not only do these duties call for advanced qualifications, but also the potential consequence of error is considerable.

(2) Accuracy as a classification factor is **not** present in the position of the clerk who files book cards. This is a matter of carefulness.

Responsibility for public contacts -- This responsibility varies as to extent, difficulty, and importance from position to position and may be worthy of consideration in classification. Evaluation of its importance depends upon a number of elements: (1) the various classes of the public to be dealt with; (2) the scope and difficulty of the activity to be presented; (3) the purposes of the contacts to be made; (4) the importance of their accomplishment; (5) the degree of authority vested in the employee; and (6) the extent to which this authority is subject to supervision.

Example:

The clerk at the circulation desk charging books has some responsibility for public contacts, but it is obvious, in the light of the above elements, that it is slight when compared to the librarian who sells the services of his library to the community, defends a budget, inaugurates discussion groups, or contacts publicity outlets.

Supervisory and Administrative Responsibilities

Supervisory and administrative responsibilities involve the administering, directing, and overseeing of the work of others. The positions containing these responsibilities vary considerably in their supervisory elements. One may deal chiefly with overseeing the work of employees in such matters as assignments, work methods, and results. Another may deal with various phases of planning, having little or no responsibility for work methods and techniques. A third and higher level may be responsible for the administration of the entire organization, including broad phases of policy and the carrying out of these policies as a whole.

Supervisory and administrative responsibilities may cover any or all of the following in varying combinations and degrees:

Policies -- The range may extend through several levels from the recommendation or determination of a policy at its inception to its interpretation and application in the various departments.

Planning -- This may begin with the establishment of ways and means for accomplishing the purposes of the organization as a whole and move downward to the determination of techniques and details for a single job.

Flow of work -- This covers the course of the work from its beginning to its completion. Responsibility may range from general planning of the work sequence through the whole organization to the arranging for the work flow through a group of departments, a single department, or a single position.

"Housekeeping" management -- This covers such matters as personnel management, expenditures, supplies, equipment, floor space, and departmental arrangement. The responsibility is usually shared and is directed downward from a department chief to successive lower positions. It ranges from positions where general regulations are established and ultimate decisions are made to the intermediate supervisory positions empowered only to make recommendations and minor decisions.

Review of work -- "Reviewing" or "revising" work means the critical examination of something initiated by someone else. Types of review vary from the proofreading of copy typed by another for the elimination of typographical errors to the final checking of a piece of work for the accuracy and completeness of facts, and for the validity of the conclusions reached and the action taken. This responsibility also carries the authority to make any changes which the reviser feels are needed.

Assignments -- The selection of work for employees, the establishment of work sequence, and the selection of employees for assignments are supervisory duties. Highest responsibility rests with the administrator who has full authority over the whole. It continues on a lower level to the supervisor responsible only for the distribution of work to a single group of employees with no problem of selection being present.

Work methods -- This involves the technique of doing the work and the sequence of steps necessary to its accomplishment. Responsibility may vary considerably. In areas where the work methods are standard, responsibility for this factor is slight, but the concern is with the excellence of technique rather than the methods employed. For example, the methods of using reference materials are somewhat standardized, but these methods are not as important as the excellence of technique in using the materials.

Coordination -- This is concerned with the development and operation of procedures in order that they remain consistent throughout. Responsibility ranges from the determination of procedures over a broad area to that exercised in seeing that these established procedures are being followed.

Production -- The amount of work done and the promptness of its accomplishment are supervisory responsibilities. They range from administrative matters of broad scope, such as the development of incentives for the entire staff, to the direct supervision of work production within a single small group.

For classification purposes, the above types of supervision must be considered as well as the degree to which they are present in each position. In addition, there are other factors which have bearing on the classification of the position. These are: (1) the extent to which the initiative of those supervised is limited; (2) the number and type of positions supervised; and (3) the level of difficulty and variety of functions supervised.

The limitation of initiative -- Supervisory control requires consideration from two standpoints, that of the supervisor and that of the supervised. In cases where the initiative of those supervised is limited, the control is vested in the supervisory position. In other cases where authority over certain matters has been delegated to the supervised positions, the supervisory positions entail less control. The factor of control must be present and as it increases in degree in one position, it decreases in the other. For classification purposes, this degree of control must be carefully studied from the original questionnaire. The varying degrees have been classed by the Civil Service Assembly under the following phrases: "Under Immediate Supervision," "Under General Supervision," "Under General Direction," and have been thoroughly and adequately described.[3]

The number and types of positions supervised -- The number of positions supervised is another factor to be considered. The larger the staff for which

---

[3] Civil Service Assembly, *op. cit.*, p.123-24.

the supervisor is responsible, the greater his responsibilities are apt to be for planning work methods, assignments, etc. Numbers should never be the sole factor, however, in determining supervisory responsibility. Consideration must also be given to the _classes_ of positions supervised. The supervisory responsibility entailed in directing a large number engaged in simple routine work may be less than that of directing a smaller group engaged in varied and/or more difficult work.

The level of difficulty and variety of functions supervised -- The level of difficulty of the functions of any unit is a relative matter, but fair judgment should be secured by comparing it with other units within the organization. The variety of functions supervised must also be considered. In a department having a complex organization and variety of functions, the supervisor must have a broader background of experience and a higher degree of administrative ability, for more difficult supervisory problems will be encountered. If positions supervised are scattered geographically, as might be in the case of a branch or extension department in a public library, or of a departmental, school, or college library in a university, this element should be considered, for more supervisory problems result.

Qualification Standards

Qualifications necessary for efficient performance of the duties of a given position are not literally factors, but they do affect classification and are useful as a measure of the other factors. Stating the qualification standards for a given position is one way of indicating the difficulty and complexity of its duties and responsibilities. Thus, the difficulty of a task may be measured by the following factors: (1) experience necessary for its efficient performance; (2) education and training essential as a foundation for that experience; and (3) basic traits and abilities necessary to acquire the skill and knowledge required for that task.

Care must be taken in determining these qualification standards. There may be a tendency to expect the position to require the qualifications of its present incumbent, though these may be above or below those really essential to the position. Another common error is to set the qualifications higher than those actually required for the position. This usually arises because of the feeling that a certain classification, and, therefore, its pay scale, is necessary to attract persons to the position. Unless the analyst can demonstrate, by measuring the duties and responsibilities of the position, that such qualifications are essential to its performance, there is no justification for them.

In libraries where compulsory certification laws exist or which operate under civil service, qualification requirements may necessarily be based on standards set by law. The standards given in the A.L.A. classification and pay plans[4]

---

[4] American Library Association, Board on Personnel Administration, _Classification and Pay Plans for Municipal Public Libraries_ (Chicago: American Library Assn., 1939)

American Library Association, Board on Personnel Administration, Subcommittee on Budgets, Compensation and Schemes of Service for Libraries Connected with Universities, Colleges and Teacher Training Institutions, _Classification and Pay Plans for Libraries in Institutions of Higher Education_ (2d ed.; Chicago: American Library Assn., 1947), 3v.

are those recognized by the association and should be followed, insofar as possible, by the individual library making a position-classification plan.

These four factors must be kept in mind constantly when analyzing positions for classification purposes: (1) difficulty and complexity of duties; (2) non-supervisory responsibilities; (3) supervisory and administrative responsibilities; and (4) qualification standards. Although, to the novice, it may seem a superhuman task to keep them and their various ramifications in mind at one time and to balance one against the other, the analyst finds that as he constantly refers to them, they quickly become increasingly familiar.

Chapter V

DEVELOPING THE SCHEDULE OF CLASSES

The factors in position classification discussed in the preceding section are the tools which are used in analyzing positions and later in allocating positions to specific classes. This indicates that a schedule of classes must be set up, but several steps are necessary before this process can be completed.

Analyzing Positions

The completed job specifications provide the material used in the process. If complete anonymity is desired, the analysis of positions can be made from these alone. There is, however, a definite advantage in having at hand all information concerning the job. Thus, it is better to have the questionnaire, the interview, and observation notes all attached to the specification for quick referral.

Up to this point positions have been studied by departmental or supervised units. A preliminary sorting of jobs is now made according to the kind of work irrespective of the level, thus, segregating positions into occupational groupings. In the library, it divides the professional from the nonprofessional positions, and in distinguishing between these groups, the question naturally arises as to what are the criteria for this division.

Professional positions -- These require for their adequate performance: (1) an understanding of library objectives, functions, procedures, and techniques; (2) a familiarity with principles of library organization and administration, including the interrelation of library departments; (3) acquaintance with the contents and use of basic reference tools; and (4) an understanding of books and readers, and the means by which they are brought into effective relationship. It is true that certain individual duties or operations legitimately assigned to professional level positions can be performed by clerical employees who have been taught those specific duties or operations. In most cases, however, professional judgment and background necessary for the handling of exceptions to routine should be required. Similarly, the immediate knowledge of "what-to-do-next" in situations varying from the usual pattern of activity is a factor which makes it a long-run economy to have some library processes carried through to completion by professional personnel, even though certain purely clerical or routine operations are included at one or more steps along the way. Included also in professional positions are those which require specialized knowledge in fields other than librarianship, such as public relations, personnel, and business administration.

Nonprofessional positions -- Nonprofessional positions are those in which: (1) the major proportion of duties can be suitably performed by persons without professional library education or equivalent experience, after a normal amount of training in specific routines or in the use of specific library catalogs, files, and indexes; and (2) relatively less discretion, judgment, or initiative is required to foresee and carry through varying additional steps beyond the learned routine and to handle special cases which represent exceptions to the normal procedure. These criteria do not, of course, apply to such positions as custodian, secretary, and bookkeeper. They are nonprofessional in character, but they call for specialized training or experience and require considerable discretion, judgment, and initiative.

The basic criteria for determining whether a library position requires a candidate of professional level, therefore, are not entirely the operations an individual may perform but include also a consideration of the kind and extent of background needed to carry through the entire work of the position. Even at the beginning professional level, candidates are expected to be able to assume responsibility for performing their daily duties largely on their own initiative after learning the procedures and policies of their departments, drawing on their professional background for making the independent decisions that arise in the course of their work.

Library studies on the problem of distinguishing between the professional and nonprofessional furnish valuable information. One of the most recent and helpful of these is the A.L.A. descriptive list of duties performed in libraries[1] which lists tasks under the headings of professional and nonprofessional. This study should be used by any library making an analysis and classification of positions.

It will be found that some positions will not fall clearly into either group because a mixture of professional and nonprofessional duties appear in them. The problem of classifying these mixed positions will be dealt with in the chapter, ALLOCATING POSITIONS TO SPECIFIC CLASSES. The first arrangement, even though tentative, serves as a preliminary breakdown into groups containing jobs of more or less similarity.

The levels of responsibility -- A further division is now made within these first two rough groupings, considering the relative level of each position within the group. It is here the factors in position classification, discussed in the previous section, come into use. As the individual positions are studied from job specification and questionnaire, detailed notes should be made concerning the elements in the position denoting difficulty or responsibility which will be apt to have bearing on the ultimate classification of the position.

Positions are, thus, arranged in two groupings, professional and nonprofessional, and within these groups tentatively graded by application of the factors in position classification. The analyst now begins to think in terms of a series of classes arranged from the lowest to the highest level like the steps of a ladder.

Determining Classes

One of the most important decisions in the development of a classification

---
[1] American Library Association, Board on Personnel Administration, Subcommittee on Analysis of Library Duties, Descriptive List of Professional and Nonprofessional Duties in Libraries (Preliminary draft; Chicago: American Library Assn., 1948)

plan is determining the classes of positions to be established. The definition of a class requires that positions falling in a particular class be sufficiently similar in respect to their duties and responsibilities to be given the same descriptive title, to require substantially the same qualifications, and to be accorded the same scale of pay. The question of what constitutes a "sufficient degree" of similarity is often difficult to answer and requires the exercise of sound judgment.

In some instances the establishment of classes is fairly simple. Some positions may be found to be almost identical in their duties and responsibilities and significantly different from all other positions.

Examples:

(1) A group of clerks in a circulation department may be assigned the specific and limited duties of charging and discharging books. There is no doubt that all of these positions will fall in the same class.

(2) Another group of clerks in the catalog department is assigned various duties of filing, typing, and other routines. The analyst must decide whether these positions are on the same level of difficulty and responsibility, or whether two or more levels are to be established.

Problems will inevitably arise during the development of a position-classification plan which require decisions on the breadth or narrowness of the classes being established. The degree of refinement is determined by the considerations of usefulness, clarity, and common sense. Position classification is an administrative tool. The classes which are established must, therefore, serve administrative purposes. The analyst must study the ways in which the classes will later be used in personnel and administrative operations: in recruiting and testing, promotion and transfer, training and rating employees; and in the establishment of a pay plan and the preparation of salary budgets. The analyst and the administrator should work out a plan best suited to the particular library.

Examples:

(1) If the nonprofessional positions in the catalog department, cited in the above example, are all on the same level of difficulty and responsibility, and these positions are also equal to those in the circulation department, then it must be decided whether these positions in different departments should all be in one class or in separate classes. In dealing with such routine positions as these, one all-inclusive class would probably be sufficient. If two classes are needed, there would be one for catalog clerks and one for circulation clerks.

(2) On a higher level, the problem of whether to establish one class or many may be greater. If the decision is to establish separate classes, there would be, for instance, classes for catalog librarians, children's librarians, circulation librarians, etc., even though there might be only one position in each class.

The Civil Service Assembly[2] gives a full discussion regarding the establishment of classes including a consideration of the legal requirements under Civil Service. The A.L.A. classification and pay plans[3] are valuable tools in deciding both the number of classes to be set up and the content of each. The sample classification plans, on file at A.L.A. Headquarters and available for loan, will be of help to libraries.

Selecting Class Titles

As soon as classes are determined, they are given a title in order that they may be referred to more easily. The class title is a definite name or title applied to a class and to each position in the class. The title should be: (1) descriptive of both the kind of work and the rank or level of the class; (2) consistent with the titles of the other classes; and (3) brief.

The titles as given in the A.L.A. classification and pay plans[4] are recommended for the library field. In these plans, the term, librarian, is used only for professional positions, those in the nonprofessional classes being termed clerks, stenographers, etc. The prefixes, junior, intermediate, and senior, are used for the professional positions. It is possible to omit ranking adjectives, substituting suffixed Roman numerals such as Librarian I, Librarian II, etc., but since it is ultimately necessary to convey the meaning of the numbers in descriptive words, it would seem desirable to use them in the first place.

Writing Class Definitions

With classes established and class titles selected for each, the next step is the writing of a class definition. The tentative definition may be revised after further analysis, but it serves as a working tool in allocating positions to classes. This working definition is a short statement of the work performed in the class, including the factors which differentiate that class from all others. It contains duties and responsibilities and indicates difficulty and the kind and degree of supervision.

A class definition is usually composed of few declarative clauses phrased in the present tense. The degree of supervision exercised over these positions is generally indicated in the opening clause. Such phrases as "under immediate

---

[2] Civil Service Assembly of the United States and Canada, Committee on Position-classification and Pay Plans in the Public Service, Position-classification in the Public Service (Chicago: The Assembly, 1941), p.195-205.

[3] American Library Association, Board on Personnel Administration, Classification and Pay Plans for Municipal Public Libraries (Chicago: American Library Assn., 1939)

American Library Association, Board on Personnel Administration, Subcommittee on Budgets, Compensation and Schemes of Service for Libraries Connected with Universities, Colleges and Teacher Training Institutions, Classification and Pay Plans for Libraries in Institutions of Higher Education (2d ed.; Chicago: American Library Assn., 1947), 3v.

[4] Ibid.

supervision," "under general supervision," and "under general direction," serve to denote the type of control.[5] These phrases are followed by the title of the supervising position.

The duties and responsibilities are introduced by such phrases as "to have charge of," "to plan and direct," "to assist with"; or the specific duty may be indicated as "to do reference work," "to do cataloging," "to file," and "to type." The degree of difficulty and responsibility is shown by the use of broad adjectives. To assure their consistent use throughout the classification, it is well to decide beforehand on the phrasing of their rank order. For example, difficulty of work may be indicated by this series of adjectives: (1) simplest routine; (2) of less than average difficulty; (3) of average difficulty; (4) of more than average difficulty; (5) very difficult; (6) exceptionally difficult. Supervisory responsibility is indicated by stating the size of the staff supervised. The definition of duties ends with the clause, "and to do such other work as may be required." There are two reasons for this: the statement shows that only the main tasks have been listed and it indicates that the employee may be subject to assignments other than those expressly mentioned.

Examples:

(1) <u>CHIEF CIRCULATION LIBRARIAN</u>[6]
Class A Circulation Department

Definition of the Class of Position:

Under direction of the Chief Librarian or the Associate (or Assistant) Chief Librarian, to have charge of the work of a Class A Circulation Department, i.e., having a staff of 2 to 6 full-time members (or their equivalent in part time) including the chief; and to do such other work as may be required.

(2) <u>INTERMEDIATE REFERENCE LIBRARIAN</u>[6]

Definition of the Class of Position:

Under supervision of the Chief Reference Librarian or other designated authority, to do reference work of average difficulty and responsibility and of a character calling for the application of modern library techniques; and to do such other work as may be required.

<u>Setting up Classification Grades</u>

Classification grades are groupings of classes according to their relative

---

[5] See Civil Service Assembly, op. cit., p.123-24.
[6] These examples have been taken from American Library Association, Board on Personnel Administration, Subcommittee on Budgets . . ., op. cit., Vol. 3, Universities, p.47 and p.97. Class definitions given in these A.L.A. plans may serve as models for individual libraries.

difficulty and responsibility. All classes in the same grade should be substantially equal in respect to difficulty and responsibility, even though these classes vary widely in character, subject matter, or function. They must also require the same basic qualifications and call for the same rate of pay. In the example described on page 29, the decision may be made to place the catalog librarian, the circulation librarian, the children's librarian, etc., in separate classes, because their functions and the kind of required experience and qualifications are different. If, however, the amount of experience, the type of qualifications, and the level of responsibilities and duties are the same, all these classes should be placed in the same grade. The sole purpose of classification grades is to provide a handy tool. In a small library where there will be few classes and where only one or two positions will be in one class, it is very questionable whether it is necessary to group classes into grades, since the number of classes is not unwieldy.

Thus, finally, step by step, the description of positions has been reduced to uniform and comparable terminology, classes have been set up into which the positions may be allocated, and grades provided to complete the classification structure.

Making Known to Employees the Tentative Classification Grades, Class Titles, and Definitions

As previously pointed out, it is important for the employees to be informed at all times of the progress of the survey. With classes and grades tentatively selected, class titles assigned, and definitions written, this information should be given to all employees. This may be done by summarizing the tentative plan in an informational bulletin or by posting it on bulletin boards. If possible, a preliminary edition of the plan should be distributed. The employee is, thus, introduced to the classification scheme, and comparisons may be made with old schedules, if they exist. He can visualize how his own job might fit into the whole and see its relationship to other positions in the entire classification plan. Group meetings or an open hearing should be held after the employees have studied the plan. This allows for democratic participation and the asking and answering of questions on an open and fair basis. The analysts should also invite employees to come and discuss privately any questions they might have. Since many questions are apt to revolve around the individual's own place in the scheme, he might hesitate to bring them up in a group meeting.

Chapter VI

ALLOCATING POSITIONS TO SPECIFIC CLASSES

Tentatively Allocating Positions to Classes

Although the steps of analyzing positions, determining classes and grades, selecting class titles, and writing class definitions have been discussed separately, actually, one step is not completed before another is begun. Since the number and description of classes are based on the individual positions as analyzed, and the lines of demarcation between the classes cannot be determined fully until all positions falling in that class are identified, the recognition of classes and the allocation of positions to classes are simultaneous operations. A tentative allocation of positions to classes is made by placing together all questionnaires or job specifications which are, by application of the factors in position classification, similar in difficulty and complexity of duties, nonsupervisory responsibilities, supervisory responsibilities, and qualification standards.

Following is an example of how the factors of position classification are applied to the job specification of the junior reference librarian. (For the SAMPLE JOB DESCRIPTION of this position see p. 78.)

Example:

In the first analysis of positions, a preliminary sorting was made according to the kind of work. When the requisites for professional and nonprofessional positions (see p. 27-28) are applied to the job specification of the junior reference librarian (see p. 17 and 78), it is obvious that this is a professional position. Further assurance may be given, however, by checking each task on the job specification with the A.L.A. descriptive list of duties.[1] Under "Reference Work - Professional Duties" we find the items: "Answering reference questions"; "Organizing and maintaining information files"; "Making special indexes"; "Compiling bibliographies"; and "Verifying bibliographical data for interlibrary loans." The job specification for this position adds to this last item "and keeping these records." Under "Registration and Circulation - Nonprofessional Duties" we find "Maintaining interlibrary loan records." This item is then a combination of professional and nonprofessional duties. The task, "Ordering, checking, and filing government documents," does not appear as such in the A.L.A. list. In the interview it was found that the _selection_ of these documents was not a part of this position. In the A.L.A. list under "Acquisition of Material - Nonprofessional Duties" items of ordering and checking appear. It is then a safe deduction that this item is nonprofessional. By adding the percentage of

---

[1] American Library Association, Board on Personnel Administration, Subcommittee on Analysis of Library Duties, _Descriptive List of Professional and Nonprofessional Duties in Libraries_ (Preliminary draft; Chicago: American Library Assn., 1948)

time spent on each professional task and comparing it with the total time spent on nonprofessional tasks, it is established that the position is predominantly professional in "kind" of work.

In order to determine the relative level of this position within a group of positions (see p. 30), the factors of position classification (see p. 18-26) are applied. Detailed notes are made on each factor indicating the elements of difficulty and responsibility which will likely have a bearing on the classification of the position.

1. Difficulty and Complexity of Duties
    (See p. 18-20 for the discussion of these factors.)

    a. How far work has progressed -- In order to determine this element, the other positions in the reference department must be studied. There is no indication in this job specification that the employee did not usually carry the tasks through from their inception to completion. Therefore, this element is present to a fairly large degree.

    b. How work is assigned -- The employee takes all questions in turn - information, research, etc., so there is no selection of work in the assignments. Over a period of time the questions represent various degrees of difficulty, thus, this element of difficulty carries some weight.

    c. Procedure followed by the employee -- There is not any great opportunity to initiate plans or actions in this position, but since the alert employee may suggest indexes and files which are needed or better ways of making or maintaining such files, the procedure should be investigated by the analyst. The decisions made are in regard to the proper reference tool to use in searching for the answer to questions. A study of the work done in the position reveals a rather high degree of mental ability required.

    d. Relationship of one employee's work to others -- The questionnaire indicated the type of supervision received. This was transferred to the job description as "under the general supervision of the chief of the reference department." Therefore, the supervision of this position is not detailed. Since the employee carries through with most of his tasks, there is also little relationship with the work of others.

    e. Variety and scope of duties -- The duties in this position are rather closely connected, all depending upon a knowledge of reference methods and practices and acquaintance with reference tools. Although the variety and scope of duties are limited, the level of difficulty of the tasks is relatively high.

2. Nonsupervisory Responsibilities
    (See p. 20-23 for the discussion of these factors.)

    a. Independence of action and decision -- This position contains considerable independence of action and decision in regard to the searching for and giving of reference information. A test of this independence is the amount of control or supervision from above. Since the control over this position is general rather than immediate, independence of action and decision is relatively high.

b. Responsibility for recommending plans and policies -- This responsibility is slight when compared with the examples on pages 21-22. The analyst, however, should investigate to see how much of this responsibility is placed in the position by the chief of the department.

c. Responsibility for money, supplies, equipment -- Since money is not handled at all, and equipment and supplies are limited to the use of files, typewriter, etc., this element of responsibility is slight.

d. Responsibility for accuracy -- This element is present to a rather high degree, since the junior reference librarian has ultimate responsibility for giving correct information. Accuracy in this respect is dependent upon advanced qualifications and is required to such a degree as to be difficult of attainment.

e. Responsibility for public contacts -- This element is present when the employee deals with patrons in the department, but it is not great, because planning for formal contacts is not present.

3. Supervisory and Administrative Responsibilities
(See p. 23-25 for the discussion of these factors.)

The responsibilities in regard to Policies, Planning, Flow of work, "Housekeeping" management, Review of work, Assignments, Work methods, Coordination, and Production are present in this position only insofar as the chief of the department may consult the employee in regard to them. The ultimate responsibility rests with the chief of the department, so this factor is not a classification consideration in the position being analyzed.

4. Qualification Standards
(See p. 25-26 for the discussion of these factors.)

The qualifications listed on the job specification for this position indicated a high level of education, specialized skills and abilities, and exacting personality traits. Experience is not a factor since no previous experience was required.

Mixed positions -- As it has been pointed out, some positions are very easily classified, the duties remaining substantially the same month after month, and the duties and responsibilities being on practically the same level. Many positions, however, present a difficult problem because the duties and responsibilities vary from time to time[2] or they are of different levels of

---
[2] Exceptional, emergency, or incidental assignments should be eliminated from classification consideration and a sufficiently long view taken to obtain the continuing duties in the position.

difficulty. Such positions are called "mixed."

Example:

The SAMPLE JOB DESCRIPTION of the desk assistant (p. 76) points up tasks which are of different levels of difficulty and responsibility. This position is predominantly nonprofessional in "kind" of work. The tasks of "Assisting readers to locate and select books" and "Giving talks on books and reading" are professional, however, as is the planning part of the bulletin board work. This makes a total of about 20% professional, and the rest nonprofessional.

In this example, if the nonprofessional items occupied 100% of the time of this employee, the position would be classified as nonprofessional. If the professional items occupied the full working time, the position would be classified as professional. The question is - Which duties and responsibilities of the position govern its classification?

The general rule to be followed in the classification of mixed positions is that the duties and responsibilities which occupy the major part of the employee's time are the basis for its classification. Occasionally an exception is made to this rule, and the highest type of duty performed may govern the classification. This exception should be made only when the governing duty is so markedly different from the other duties of the position as to be a basis for recruiting and to require unquestionably higher qualifications.

After the initial classification has been adopted, mixed positions may well be analyzed for the purpose of reassignment of duties. It may be found that several positions classified in professional grades carry a fairly large percentage of time spent on clerical tasks. This may indicate that, by reassignment of duties, these positions can be filled by fewer professional employees plus some full-time nonprofessional help. This reassignment is an administrative problem brought to light by the survey, but is mentioned here because the analyst should be aware of these discrepancies and make notes concerning them.

Examples:

(1) The analyses of the positions of two catalog librarians reveal that each contains roughly 50% of the time spent on actually cataloging and 50% on typing cards. A reassignment of duties would make one position 100% professional cataloging and the second position 100% nonprofessional typing.

(2) On the other hand, although the positions of two professional employees in the circulation department may reveal that 50% of the time is spent in routines and the other 50% on actually assisting patrons, it may be necessary to retain the two positions on a professional basis because long hours of service and a small staff require the professional personnel to be spread thinly to cover schedules.

Position comparisons -- Positions are never considered as isolated units, thus, they must be compared with each other in order to observe the differences and similarities and to determine the relationships among them. The factors of difficulty and responsibility are relative and their gradations are established by comparing them in the various positions. Comparisons also reveal the interrelation of positions as a result of the flow of work and reveal the element of supervision received or exercised in the position.

Example:

Compare the junior reference librarian position with the chief of circulation position. (For the SAMPLE JOB DESCRIPTION of these positions, see p. 77-78.)

In comparing these positions, differences and similarities are noted.

Under Difficulty and Complexity of Duties (see p. 18-20) the items, How far work has progressed and How work is assigned, are on about the same level in both positions. The item, Procedure followed by the employee, is present to a greater extent in the circulation position, since there is greater opportunity to initiate plans or actions and to make decisions. The item, Relationship of one employee's work to others, is a little greater in the department chief, since the supervision exercised by the chief librarian over this position is a little more remote than that exercised by the chief of the reference department over the junior reference librarian. The item, Variety and scope of duties, carries more weight in the circulation position, since there is considerably more variety and wider scope of duties, and the level of difficulty of most of these tasks is high.

Under Nonsupervisory Responsibilities (see p. 20-23) the items, Independence of action and decision and Responsibility for accuracy, are on about the same level in both positions. The item, Responsibility for recommending plans and policies, is slightly stronger in the circulation position, but the principal responsibility for plans and policies lies more in the supervisory factor rather than in this nonsupervisory area. In the item, Responsibility for money, supplies, equipment, the responsibility for fine money increases this factor slightly in the circulation position. In the handling of complaints and in the giving of talks to outside groups, the item, Responsibility for public contacts, is present to a considerably larger degree in the circulation position.

The greatest dissimilarity between these two positions comes in the Supervisory and Administrative Responsibilities (see p. 23-25). Almost negligible in the reference position, it is strong in all the elements of this factor in the circulation position.

In regard to Qualification Standards (see p. 25-26), a requirement of experience and such traits as the ability to organize and direct the work of others are added for the circulation position which are not a part of the requirements of the reference position.

This comparison may further be shown by graphic means. All jobs within a particular department can be ranked or listed on a vertical chart, placing the job requiring the heaviest responsibilities and most difficult duties at the top and ranging the various jobs down in the order of decreasing responsibility. This is done for each department. The departmental rankings are then placed on a comparison chart with a vertical column for each department. This chart, thus, shows the relative ranking of positions within a department and the relative equality of positions in the various departments. It is also possible to group these jobs horizontally at various levels of difficulty, responsibility, and qualification requirements, thus, indicating how classification grades may be attached.

Example:

Circulation	Reference	Catalog
Chief	Chief	Chief
Readers' Advisor	Junior Reference Librarian	Catalog Librarian
Desk Assistant		
		Catalog Clerk

A final check on allocations -- When the analyst has reviewed all positions in terms of the classification factors and allocated them to classes, these allocations are as correct as he can make them without some outside help. He now turns to supervisors to clarify or supplement the facts and to verify the tentative classification of the position. In case questions are raised concerning the classification, more information may be secured in another interview with the employee or by further observation of his work. As a result of this additional information, it may be necessary to revise the allocation.

Writing Class Specifications

With all positions allocated to classes, a class specification is written to cover all positions in a particular class. (See SAMPLE CLASS SPECIFICATIONS, p. 79-81.) This is a statement describing the work of the entire class and contains: (1) the class title; (2) the definition of the duties of the class; (3) examples of typical tasks; and (4) minimum qualifications necessary to perform the work of the class. The class title and definition have previously been established for each class. (See sections: Selecting Class Titles and Writing Class Definitions, p. 30-31.)

Typical tasks -- These must be carefully selected from the job specifications of individual positions in the class. In classes containing many positions, a selection of typical tasks may be used as illustrative. They are chosen with these questions in mind: Why do they fall in this class and not in another? and, What distinguishes them from similar tasks which fall in other classes?

Descriptions of typical tasks must be concrete and precise. If the definition of duties in the class definition has used "simplest routine," "of less than average difficulty," etc., the examples of tasks should illustrate the levels represented by these terms.

Minimum qualifications -- Minimum qualifications mentioned in connection with the job specifications are now further clarified to cover all positions in the class. They must be consistent with and derived from the duties and responsibilities of these positions.

The skills, knowledge, abilities, and personality traits which the employee must have, in order to perform effectively the work in a given class of positions, are part of the standards to be considered. They should be expressed as precisely as possible. For example, "ability to plan, lay out, direct, and coordinate the work of others" is preferable to "ability to organize." Such terms as "ability to," "proficiency in," and "skill in" may be used and may be modified by such adjectives as "demonstrated," "marked," or "outstanding" to show gradation. Degree or amount of knowledge required can be indicated by "some knowledge of" for the lowest level, to "comprehensive and detailed special knowledge" for the highest. Only those personality requirements which have a direct bearing on the job are listed. Such qualities as honesty, integrity, and industry are desirable for any class, and so are not mentioned. The quality is defined to show reason for its inclusion. For example, "genuine liking for children" is a part of the specification for a children's librarian.

The education, training, and experience requirements are also a part of the qualification standards. They indicate the background needed to be eligible for a class and suggest the likeliest source of supply from which qualified candidates can be drawn. Substitution of experience for formal education may be provided by such a phrase as "or equivalent qualifications." This implies that gradual development through increasing responsibility and experience may be substituted for formal education.

Statements regarding experience stress the _kind_ and _level_ as well as the length of that experience; for example, "four years of professional experience in a library of recognized standing, two of which have been in children's work." The length of experience may also be described by such terms as "some," "considerable," or "extensive."

Physical standards may be a part of the qualification statements if special physical stamina is a requirement of the position or positions in a class; for example, "to carry heavy loads of books," "to stand for long periods," or "to be exposed for long periods to all types of weather."

Where certificates or licenses are required, they should also be a part of the qualification statement.

Reviewing and Publishing Class Specifications

The class specifications are now subject to review and criticism by supervisors and administrators who will bear the responsibility for all final allocations and for the ultimate form of the classification plan. This review will assure that the specifications are technically sound and that they are consistent both as to content and phraseology.

This step completed, the class specifications are published and made readily available to all employees, and explanation is given as to what the specification is intended to include and exclude. It should be pointed out that examples of work are illustrative only, not complete or exclusive. Here again, it is important to explain the effect of the statement of qualifications in their relation to present incumbents.

Notifying Employees of Allocations

Preparatory to notifying the employee of his allocation, the entire classification plan is released,[3] so he may see the relationship of his position to all others in the classification structure. The importance of this step cannot be overemphasized, for the employee has no way of judging the fairness of where his job has been placed unless he can compare it with others. If the whole picture is not revealed, suspicion and fear grow quickly, for the employee can never be certain that other positions are not rated higher than his, even though the exact opposite may be true.

An individual notice should then be sent to each employee, showing the allocation of the position which he occupies. An explanatory note should accompany the notice, stating that the allocations represent the recommendations of supervisors, administrators, and analysts; that they relate to positions and not to persons; that any employee who believes that the allocation of his position is incorrect should discuss his problem with the analyst; and, if he is still not satisfied, he should file a written statement to that effect with the administrator before a stated date, giving his reasons. Thus, he is given an opportunity for appeal and review of his case. In a small library, notification and provision for appeal might be done privately with each employee.

Adjusting Disagreements

Those responsible for the classification should consider all questions and statements of dissatisfaction, then hold individual conferences with these employees. The employee should be given full opportunity to present his case. The analysts then review the duties and responsibilities involved in the position and set forth the factors upon which the allocation was based. The effect of possible decisions on other positions should be made clear. After these conferences, reinvestigation may be necessary and may result in changes in the allocation lists. All employees filing statements should be notified promptly in writing of the final decisions.

After adjustments have been made, allocation lists are published showing the class to which each position in the service has been allocated. This may be done by class of positions or by departments.

Adopting the Position-classification Plan

The final step in a position-classification survey is the adoption of the plan by the governing body. In order that the plan may be presented to it with

---

[3] If a salary schedule (see Chapter VIII) has been worked out concurrently with the classification plan, salary ranges for each class should also be made public.

a recommendation of adoption from the library employees as a whole, it is advisable to secure this recommendation first. Full explanation should be made concerning the basis and structure of the plan, and needs for and benefits of it should be reviewed. While procedure for adoption varies with the local situation, some formal action should be taken by the governing body before the position-classification plan is actually installed. The allocation lists are also adopted officially. The plan is now ready to be put into operation.

Chapter VII

INSTALLATION AND ADMINISTRATION OF THE POSITION-CLASSIFICATION PLAN

After the plan has been formally adopted, certain provisions must be made for its installation, its administration, and for keeping it current. There are also problems involved in adapting a new plan to an existing one. In order to discuss these provisions and problems, it is well to consider how a position-classification plan is used in administration.

Using the Plan in Administration

A position-classification plan provides a sound foundation for all phases of personnel management. It becomes: (1) an aid in the establishment of a pay plan and the preparation of salary budgets; (2) a personnel tool for recruiting and testing, promotion and transfer, training and rating employees; (3) a help in planning and improving organization; and (4) a factor in the promotion of better employee-management relations.

Pay plans and salary budgets -- Equity is the goal of a good pay plan. Under the same employment conditions, employees doing work of equal difficulty and responsibility should be on the same pay scale. The classification of positions according to the difficulty and responsibility of the work, thus, provides a sound basis for achieving this goal of equity. It is only by comparison of the work of one position with others that relative values can be determined and suitable salary scales set.

Names of positions have meaning only when they are used uniformly and are accompanied by clear-cut definitions. In the absence of a position-classification plan, the same name may be used to refer to different kinds of positions since the exact position content is not defined. Under a classification plan, budget schedules are built upon the official class titles, each clearly defined in the class specification.

A personnel tool -- With its orderly arrangement of facts about duties, responsibilities, and qualifications, the classification plan is useful in recruiting employees; and the job specification, indicating the work involved and the qualifications required for the position, can be sent to an employment agency as a complete picture of the position to be filled. Class specifications, showing required qualifications, greatly facilitate the preparation of tests for the selection of personnel and make possible the use of only one test to cover all positions in a single class rather than a large variety of tests for similar individual positions.

Class specifications also point the way to the selection of the person with the proper background of training and experience for promotion and transfer, and the whole classification plan is a foundation for a logical and fair promotion policy. With classes arranged in varying degrees of difficulty and responsibility, promotion from one class to another is clearly outlined for administrators and employees alike.

Before a training program can be set up, there must be an analysis and a description of the work for which the employee is to be trained. Moreover, the efficiency of the person doing each job is more accurately evaluated when the standards of the individual jobs are clearly established. Thus, the job description and the job specification supply vital information for training and rating employees.

Planning and improving organization -- Good organization in the library involves the relating of efforts and abilities, and the arranging of personnel and departments in such a way as to produce the best possible service at minimum cost and effort. In order to achieve this goal, a continuing survey must be made of the duties and responsibilities of positions, their supervisory relationships, and the flow of work among them. All of these facts are disclosed in the position-classification survey.

Representative of the flaws in organization which may be revealed in such a survey are: (1) duplication of work; (2) confusion in the delegation of authority; (3) gaps in responsibilities; (4) unnecessary operations; (5) poor work methods; (6) improper assignment of duties; (7) lack of coordination among departments; (8) rough work flow; and (9) too broad a span of administrative control. The discovery of such flaws is an important by-product of position classification.

Employee-management relations -- The classification plan has a definite contribution to make in improving employee morale. It analyzes and classifies jobs, not people, thus, it is objective and impersonal. It provides a foundation for uniformity and equity of action in the many phases of personnel administration. In determining lines of promotion and defining potential career avenues, it can be an incentive for advancement. By clarifying the content of the job and its relationship to other positions, it enables the employee to see the importance of his own work and the part it plays in the whole organization.

Providing for the Installation and Administration of the Plan

It is an administrative problem to see that the position-classification plan is properly installed and continues to operate. This can be done only if a person or group of persons, endowed with the necessary authority, are designated to perform this function, and a set of rules is formulated for the operation of the plan.

The agency to administer the plan -- The agency which is charged with the selection, training, and placing of personnel is the logical one to administer the classification plan. In organizations having a personnel department, this duty would naturally rest with that department. In libraries operating under civil service, the commission and a library representative might perform this work. In smaller libraries, the chief librarian may feel that he can administer the plan. The busy administrator, however, may not find time to carry through, and the plan soon becomes obsolete. One solution is to have a committee representing employees and administration carry out this duty. If an employee committee has been used in conducting the position-classification survey, members of that group should certainly be retained on this continuing committee because of the valuable background they would bring to it. The final responsibility for classification administration, however, always rests with the chief librarian.

The agency which has been selected to carry out this work has all data thus far collected turned over to it. These consist of notes on preliminary planning, questionnaires, job descriptions, interview notes, job specifications, and an official copy of the classification plan including class specifications and allocation lists.

Rules for the installation and administration of the plan -- In large libraries, formal rules[1] should be set up for the installation and continued administration of the plan. These usually consist of an introductory section defining the terms used in the plan, an interpretation of the class specifications, an official copy of the position-classification plan, rules concerning the initial allocation of positions, the change of allocations as a result of reclassification, and provision for appeals. They should also state the procedure for requesting a reclassification and provide for a periodic review of the plan at stated intervals. Smaller libraries will probably not feel the need for such formal rules. In all cases, however, an official copy of the plan should be maintained together with some statements regarding its installation and administration. These statements should include the effective date of adoption and an indication that after this date, new class titles are to be used and all positions allocated to their appropriate classes on the basis of duties and responsibilities. Provision should also be made concerning the qualification standards as set up and the possession or lack of them by present staff members. If, for administrative reasons, certain positions have been dealt with contrary to the precepts of the plan,[2] these exceptions should be noted in the rules.

The beginning of the calendar or the fiscal year is usually selected for the installation of the plan, and at this time the transition from the old to the new is made. New class titles are entered on all personnel and fiscal records. Recruiting, testing, promotion, and transfer of personnel and the preparation of budgets and pay plans are now done on the basis of the new classification plan.

Problems Involved in Adapting a New Plan to an Existing One

Although the emphasis throughout the survey has been on positions rather than people, the final step in putting a new classification plan into effect involves more than the impersonal word, position. Consideration of the person occupying that position becomes imperative, since the class to which each position is finally assigned inevitably affects the incumbent and his relationship to other members of the staff.

---

[1] An example of such rules is given in Civil Service Assembly of the United States and Canada, Committee on Position-classification and Pay Plans in the Public Service, Position-classification in the Public Service (Chicago: The Assembly, 1941), p.387-91.

[2] An example of this problem will be discussed under SALARY SCHEDULING - Placing the Classified Positions on the Scale (see p. 55-56).

In discussing the topic, Presenting the Idea to Those Concerned (see p. 5), it was recommended that assurance be given that no reduction in salary would be made as a result of the classification and that rankings would be maintained if possible. If the administrator had made no such promises, his problems of installation would be easily solved. Individuals would automatically fit into the grades in which the actual work involved in their positions placed them, regardless of whether this lowered their rank or salary. Those people not having the minimum qualifications required for their positions would be transferred to positions carrying qualifications which they could meet.

Without such assurance, the entire survey would be doomed to failure at the outset, for employees would probably not tell the whole truth about their jobs, and supervisors, fearful of their own situations, would shield employees rather than aid in finding the truth. The analyst, who must depend upon the cooperation of the individual to obtain a true picture of the job, would be faced with suspicion, fear, and a guarded exterior impossible to penetrate.

The administrator should promise that, as a result of the survey itself: (1) no salaries will be cut; (2) individuals will be considered to have the qualifications called for by the positions they occupy; and (3) every attempt will be made to preserve the present ranking and prestige of the staff members.

The salary problem -- When a salary schedule is applied to the classification plan, it will probably be found that a few people are already receiving salaries higher than their positions warrant. The treatment of such cases will be dealt with in Chapter VIII, SALARY SCHEDULING, in the section, Placing the Classified Positions on the Scale (see p. 55-56). It is more than likely, however, that a good many salaries will be below the schedule. This becomes a budget problem, and, if funds can be obtained to meet these salaries, the adoption of the schedule will contribute immeasurably to staff morale.

The qualification problem -- Some individuals may lack the minimum qualifications for their present positions. People in such positions, who have performed all the essentials of the job, should be considered as having the required qualifications.[3] To demote an employee in salary or position because of the lack of these newly established qualifications is one of the quickest ways to break staff morale. It should be clearly explained that after the new plan goes into effect, vacancies will be filled, whether by promotion or from outside sources, only by people having the required qualifications. Time eventually takes care of this problem, but in the interim, the individual should be accorded all the rights and privileges of his grade.

Some staff members may be found to have qualifications higher than those required by their positions. As only minimum qualifications are stated in the plan, this is not an immediate problem. As opportunities arise, every effort

---

[3] This is a discussion of qualifications only and not a discussion of ability. If the person in the position has not fulfilled the obligations of the position, demotion may be made on the basis of merit. The two problems are different and should not be considered on the same basis.

should be made to promote such persons to positions commensurate with their qualifications. Unless their actual duties change, they must remain in the grade of their present positions, no matter how high their qualifications are.

The rank or prestige problem -- The survey will probably reveal many instances of misplaced people. For example, an individual of professional rank may be spending most of his time performing clerical tasks, or the exact opposite may be true. The reorganizing of work is the first step to be taken. With unnecessary procedures eliminated and all work relationships clarified, an attempt should then be made to shift people to positions for which they are properly qualified, a task which takes both time and patience.

It will probably be found that a few people cannot fit into the reorganization plans. They have, through the years, capably performed the jobs committed to them, but to change their work radically would only make them inefficient and unhappy. To drop such people in rank would not only be unfair to them but would also seriously impair the morale of the entire staff. It is far wiser to prepare special specifications within the plan to protect these people, earmarking these positions to be dropped and the positions assigned to their correct allocations when they become vacant.

In time of quick staff turnover, these problems are generally ironed out in a short time. When the staff remains static, the process takes longer, but the wise administrator will make the "perfect" schedule his blueprint for the future. He will move towards that schedule whenever opportunity presents itself, but in the meantime, he will choose a happy staff in preference to perfection.

Keeping the Plan Current

As soon as a classification plan is adopted, its revision to meet changing conditions must be undertaken. With the development and change in library programs and policies, work methods and work flow are revised, unnecessary and duplicated operations eliminated, authorities redelegated, responsibilities redistributed, and assignments changed. This results in an alteration of position content, the abolishment of existing positions, and the establishment of new positions. Other changes are brought about by the influence exercised upon a given position by its incumbent. An exceptionally capable employee may gradually add responsibilities to his job which have come to him by virtue of his ability, thus, altering the principal emphasis of his position. Changes in one position may affect the work responsibilities of related positions. The creation of new supervisory positions may also result in the modification of responsibility of subordinate positions. In order to keep abreast of these changes, a continuous revision of the plan is necessary.

Most requests for review of positions will probably come from supervisors, as they are usually responsible for the changes that have occurred through changes in assignments. Individual employees, however, also report changes in their positions and request a review of their classification. Since supervisors and employees may readily report changes likely to result in raising their classification, but may be reluctant to divulge information which might lead to a lowering of status, the classification agency must be constantly alert to discover changes on its own initiative.

Reclassification procedure -- The procedure for reclassifying a position is the same as that used in its original classification. Duties and responsibilities are analyzed and evaluated by means of a new questionnaire and interview, then compared with the original data. If the position is given a new allocation, the class specification into which it now falls should be reviewed for possible additions in typical tasks listed, and its former specification should be checked for possible deletions.

New or changed positions may be so different from others in the library that they are not covered by the existing classification plan. It then becomes necessary to alter the plan itself, adding new classes or reconstructing existing classes. This might occur when a department engages in a distinctly new activity, or when phases of work previously performed in several positions are consolidated into one position. In general, however, it is preferable to try to fit new positions into the present scheme if at all possible.

Revision of classes may also be occasioned by difficulties encountered in using them in recruiting and testing. Classes may be found to be too broad or too narrow for easy use in these activities. It is only through the use of a plan that its adequacy in serving the various uses of administration is tested.

Periodic review -- Effective administration of any position-classification plan depends upon periodic review of the entire scheme. This should be done at least every five years in order that the plan may adequately describe all positions as they currently exist. In case an outside agency has made the original survey, it should probably be engaged to conduct periodic reviews, since it is familiar with the situation.

The periodic review is conducted in precisely the same way that the initial position-classification survey is made. All the steps outlined in this manual from Presenting the Idea to Those Concerned to Adopting the Position-classification Plan are covered. In the case of the first step, it is the need for a revision of the plan which is presented. All data gathered are compared with those obtained in the original survey, and changes made, where necessary, in allocations to classes and in class specifications.

Chapter VIII

SALARY SCHEDULING

The logical outgrowth of a position-classification plan is a salary schedule which assures "equal pay for equal work." Both of these tools are essential to effective personnel management. Classification surveys usually reveal that positions found to be substantially equal in difficulty and responsibility often carry widely differing rates of pay. In order to correct this situation, it is necessary to revise the existing salary schedule or to adopt a completely new one. This process involves: (1) the selection of an agency to prepare and administer it; (2) consideration of the factors used in establishing a salary schedule; (3) a study of the mechanics of setting such a schedule; and (4) the procedure for adopting it. In order to link the salary schedule to the classification plan, further discussions are included in this chapter on (5) placing the classified positions on the scale; (6) administering the salary schedule; and (7) keeping the salary schedule current.

Selecting the Agency

An agency must be selected to prepare and administer the salary schedule. The chief librarian may decide to handle this matter himself, but much is to be gained from having employee representatives work with him in solving the complex problems of salary administration. If they have also had experience in working on the position-classification survey, they will be of further value in this work. In libraries having a fiscal and/or a personnel director, they should certainly be included in the group charged with this function. The help of an outside agency is desirable. The personnel of such an agency can give an objective view of salaries, based on close experience with other professional, governmental and business standards. Moreover, they often succeed in establishing a higher salary scale than could be achieved by recommendations coming entirely from within the library itself.

Factors in Setting a Salary Schedule

The factors to be considered in setting a salary schedule are: (1) the relative difficulty and responsibility of the work of all classes of positions and the qualification requirements of each; (2) the rates of competing employers in other libraries and in other comparable fields, local and national; (3) the standards set by library and related associations; (4) certain economic and social conditions; and (5) the ability of the jurisdiction to pay.

Difficulty, responsibilities, and qualification requirements of the work — The factors which determined the classification of positions according to difficulty and responsibility of work automatically serve as the basis for setting a salary schedule, since it is to these classes of positions[1] that the salary

---

[1] If classification grades are used, the salaries are attached to these grades, since all classes calling for equal pay are grouped in one grade. For purposes of uniformity, the term, grades, is used throughout this chapter.

48

scales are attached. Positions in the various grades should be compared for salary relationships in terms of duties, responsibilities, and qualification requirements as they were in the original classification process.

Rates of competing employers -- Competition is a powerful agent in setting the price of any service. It is obvious that a library cannot attract and retain competent personnel unless its salaries are comparable to those offered by competing employers. Comparisons should be made with: (1) salaries paid by other local or nearby libraries for similar work; (2) library salary scales in cities considered comparable because of size and economic and social characteristics; (3) compensation of local school teachers and other faculty members; (4) salaries of other public employees in the community; (5) compensation paid for work in comparable occupations; and (6) local salaries paid for comparable work by private employers. For nonprofessional positions, comparisons are usually made on the local level only. The prevailing rate should generally be adopted, providing it allows a proper balance with the salaries of other positions in the plan. It must be remembered, however, that to make a satisfactory comparison in regard to salaries, it is necessary to know also the job content and responsibilities of the positions.

Standards set by library and related associations -- Minimum salary schedules have been recommended by the A.L.A. Board on Personnel Administration and adopted by the A.L.A. Council.[2] The relationships of these salaries to classification grades and qualifications may be obtained by a study of the A.L.A. classification and pay plans.[3] These salaries are regarded as being proper compensation for positions of various grades, and libraries should make every effort to meet these standards. The National Education Association has recommended a fair entering standard for teachers, and various state legislatures have set minimum teachers' salaries. All of these standards serve as guides in establishing a local salary schedule.

Economic and social conditions -- Economic and social conditions which affect salary scales include the relative cost of living in the local area and employee benefits which are allowed. In comparing salary schedules with other libraries, the U. S. Bureau of Labor Statistics Consumers' Price Index should be used for comparative living cost statistics in these cities. Employee benefits which affect salary policies include such items as pension plans, length of vacation with pay, sick leave provisions, sabbatical leave, hours of work, and expenses to conferences. Although these benefits deserve consideration,

---

[2] See "Minimum Library Salary Standards for 1951," A.L.A. Bulletin, XLV (March 1951), 102-103.

[3] American Library Association, Board on Personnel Administration, Classification and Pay Plans for Municipal Public Libraries (Chicago: American Library Assn., 1939)

American Library Association, Board on Personnel Administration, Subcommittee on Budgets, Compensation and Schemes of Service for Libraries Connected with Universities, Colleges and Teacher Training Institutions, Classification and Pay Plans for Libraries in Institutions of Higher Education (2d ed.; Chicago: American Library Assn., 1947), 3v.

they should not hold too much weight, for the presence of pension plans and of liberal allowance for vacations and leaves cannot compensate for inadequate salaries. The absence of such benefits, however, may be an influence in seeking higher salaries.

Ability of the jurisdiction to pay -- In the final analysis, the ability of the jurisdiction to pay is the most important factor in establishing a salary schedule. While other factors must be considered, the fact remains that the rates to be set must be geared realistically to the income of the library. Before any revision of the schedule is undertaken, it is necessary to obtain definite information concerning the total amount of money which will be available for salaries and the extent to which the governing body of the library will be able to secure additional funds. Recommendations concerning the portion of the total budget which should be used for salaries have been made by the A.L.A. Board on Personnel Administration.[4]

The Mechanics of Setting a Salary Schedule

The general compensation policy having been decided upon, the next step is to set pay rates for the various grades. This procedure involves: (1) setting a rate for key positions; (2) setting rates for other positions with respect to these key positions; (3) establishing salary ranges for each grade; (4) providing for a career service; and (5) providing for cost-of-living fluctuations.

Setting a rate for key positions -- At least one key position is selected for each kind of work represented in the classification plan. The beginning position in each kind of work is often selected, since it is relatively simple in regard to duties and responsibilities and requires a minimum of education and training and no experience. Other key positions are selected on a higher level so that relationships between the different levels can be established. At this point only minimum rates are set for these key positions, and these rates are determined after a consideration of the factors involved.

Example:

Key positions which might be selected in a small or medium-sized library are:

1. The beginning professional position
2. A department chief
3. The chief librarian
4. The beginning clerical position
5. An advanced clerical position
6. The beginning custodial position

Setting rates for other positions with respect to key positions -- Salaries for all grades can now be set by comparing all positions with the key positions. The factors of difficulty and responsibility provide a measuring rod

---

[4] "Minimum Library Salary Standards for 1948," *A.L.A. Bulletin*, XLII (March 1948), 104-08.

for determining the relative levels of positions in regard to wage rates.

Although various attempts have been made to work out formulae and point systems for the grading of positions,[5] the process still remains one principally dependent upon the exercise of careful judgment. It is possible, however, to set up tentative guides for determining the relationship between the salaries of various positions. For example, it may be decided that the salary for the position of department chief in a small library should be set at a figure 15% higher than for the beginning professional position and the salary of the position of chief librarian 30% higher than that of the department chief. Once the proper relationship between salaries has been established, it remains the same unless the jobs themselves change in value. The amount of salary may change, but job relationships and the relative value of jobs are not affected. A word of caution is again repeated: It is the POSITION which is being evaluated and NOT the PERSON occupying the position.

Establishing salary ranges for each grade -- The salary range is the span between the lowest and the highest salary which can be offered for positions in a certain grade. This indicates that the salary for each grade of positions will include: (1) a minimum rate; (2) several intermediate rates; and (3) a maximum rate. The minimum rate is the starting rate, and it represents the least that should be paid for any position in a given grade. Similarly, the maximum rate should be fixed at a figure representing the most that should be paid for the work involved in that position.

The spread between the minimum and maximum rates is established upon the theory that there is a progressive increase in the value of the employee as he becomes more familiar with his work. These intermediate rates, termed salary increments, also provide a reward for increased efficiency. Increments should be made on the basis of carefully prepared merit rating sheets[6] indicating satisfactory performance, and SHOULD NEVER BE ALLOWED AUTOMATICALLY. The number of intermediate steps may depend upon the length of time it will take for a new appointee to reach maximum usefulness in a specific position. The A.L.A. salary schedule for 1951[7] is on a five-step plan for all grades except the first two clerical grades, which provide for only three steps. In a five-step plan, the employee entering at the minimum salary progresses to the maximum in four years providing his work merits an annual increase. The amount of each increment varies in the standard plan[8] from $5 per month in the lower clerical grades and from $10 in the beginning professional grade.

---

[5] A system of point evaluation developed for libraries is described in Donald E. Dickason, "Sleeves or Zigzag Lines: Salary Determination Through Fair Evaluation," College and Research Libraries, VII (July 1946), 237-42.

[6] The A.L.A. has for sale a form, Personnel Service Rating Report, and an accompanying booklet, Rating a Staff for Promotion and Demotion. The latter is a reprint of an article by Francis R. St. John in the A.L.A. Bulletin, XXXIV (December 1940), 682-87.

[7] "Minimum Library Salary Standards for 1951," op. cit.

[8] Ibid.

Example:

With a minimum salary of $3057 and an annual increment of $120, the steps are: $3177, $3297, $3417, and $3537.

There is some difference of opinion as to whether salary ranges should overlap in a series of grades. The classification plan should be set up so that promotion from one grade to the next is possible. For this reason, the minimum of any grade to which promotion might be made probably should be at least one step higher than the maximum of the next lower grade. An argument against this is that the employee who has been in a position long enough to be receiving the maximum salary is worth more in that position than he would be for some time in the new one, even though the new position carries more responsibility; and for this reason, his new salary might be the same as, or even less than, the old. It would, however, seem entirely unjustified to ask an employee to take a cut in salary for an advanced position, even though it offered him greater opportunity for advancement. One solution is for the employee being promoted to start at a salary equal to or just above his former salary.

Example:

An employee has been in a grade which carries a salary range of $4236 to $4956 and is at the maximum salary of this grade. He is promoted to the next grade, carrying a salary range of $4909 to $5749 with intermediate steps at $5119, $5329, and $5539. Following the policy of starting at the salary in the next grade which is equal to or just above his former salary, he would remain at $4956 until his increment is due, or he would be moved to the $5119 step immediately.

If ranges are to have adequate spread, it is difficult to avoid overlapping salaries, but these should be kept to a minimum.

Providing for a career service -- It has been noted previously that the classification plan should provide for promotion from one grade to the next. Another type of promotion involves no fundamental change in duties. These two types of promotion are discussed in The National Plan for Public Library Service:

"Two parallel channels of promotion should be clearly recognized . . . One is the administrative channel, in which the librarian advances from a position as an individual worker to a minor administrative post and then successively to more and more important administrative positions. But this obvious type of administrative advancement is not well adapted to the capabilities and interests of many able librarians. Another career channel of professional advancement as a subject or functional specialist must also be kept open. The expert in bibliography or cataloging, the specialist in science, in fine arts, or in other subjects, the reading specialist, the children's librarian - these and other specialists should be enabled to advance in rank and salary without assuming important administrative responsibilities."[9]

Lowell Martin also discussed this promotion problem at the institute on personnel administration at the University of Chicago in 1945:

"The career ladder in librarianship shifts from the professional to the administrative service at a fairly low level. Ambitious individuals cast about for administrative positions after a short period of professional work. This shift in the career ladder of librarianship prompts persons not qualified or anxious for administrative responsibility to seek it, with the result that many able professional librarians are misplaced in administrative positions . . . A basic need of library personnel - at least as important as higher beginning salaries - is the extension of the professional career ceiling upward to the point where the complex and responsible service and bibliographic positions . . . will be staffed by career persons at a substantial salary level. The concept of the librarian as reading expert will remain only a dream unless there is a drastic revision upward of the professional salary ceiling."[10]

This problem has been recognized in the classification plan developed at the University of California, and promotion has been provided from the lowest professional grade (L-1) to the next highest (L-2) without a change of duties:

"There are five salary steps in L-1, the top one of which is the same as the lowest step in L-2. Under the promotional plan, a competent librarian would progress in four years of satisfactory work to the fifth step of L-1, or, by re-allocation, to the first step of L-2 . . . in catalog, order, and reference work . . . there is distinction between the degrees of difficulty of duties performed and responsibility exercised, and it may be assumed that as a competent librarian acquires four years of experience he thereby acquires ability to perform work of increased difficulty and to take on additional responsibility, in which case he is normally assigned the more difficult problems, and his position itself acquires the character of L-2 allocation.

"There are positions which are not susceptible of such development . . . and such positions would remain at L-1, regardless of the experience of the incumbents."[11]

---

[9] American Library Association, Committee on Postwar Planning, *A National Plan for Public Library Service*; prepared for the Committee by Carleton B. Joeckel and Amy Winslow; with a chapter by Lowell Martin, "Planning for Libraries," No. 3 (Chicago: American Library Assn., 1948), p.117.

[10] Lowell Martin, "Toward a Qualified Postwar Library Personnel," in Chicago, University, Graduate Library School, Library Institute, *Personnel Administration in Libraries*; papers presented before the Library Institute at the University of Chicago, August 27-September 1, 1945, edited with an introduction by Lowell Martin (Chicago: Univ. of Chicago Pr., c1946), p.156.

[11] Douglas W. Bryant and Boynton S. Kaiser, "A University Library Position Classification and Compensation Plan," *Library Quarterly*, XVII (January 1947), 11-12.

Provision was further made in the University of California plan for certain nonadministrative positions "requiring subject specialization or language qualifications of a very high order"[12] to be classified in L-3 which, for the most part, consists of administrative positions.

Anyone making a salary schedule should be fully aware of this problem and should make every effort to provide this career channel of promotion in one way or another.

Providing for cost-of-living adjustments -- The pay plan should consist of two parts: (1) a basic salary schedule; and (2) a cost-of-living adjustment superimposed upon the basic schedule. The purchasing power of the salary of the basic schedule fluctuates with the increases and decreases in living costs. The cost-of-living adjustment is added in time of high prices and is decreased as living costs decline, in order to assure the purchasing power represented by the original basic schedule. The base rates which were adopted by the A.L.A. Council in 1946 were geared to the 1935-1939 "Cost-of-Living Index" of 100.[13] The 1951 schedule was built on this basic schedule with a percentage added for the increased cost of living. Since the same percentage increase throughout would add much greater amounts in the upper brackets than in the lower, the amount varies in this schedule from 45.6% in the lower grades to 27.3% in the highest grades. There is room for argument as to the exact place at which the percentage should change from 45.6 to 42.3, 37.3, 32.3, and 27.3. The recommended plan, however, has been worked out to maintain a proper relationship of grades to each other.

Examples:

(1) On a $2100-$2580 range, a 45.6% increase over the minimum rate adds $957 to all steps on the scale, resulting in a $3057-$3537 span.

(2) On a $3450-$4290 range, a 42.3% increase adds $1459 to all steps on the scale, resulting in a $4909-$5749 span.

(3) On a $4800-$6000 range, a 37.3% increase adds $1790 to all steps on the scale, resulting in a $6590-$7790 span.[14]

Cost-of-living adjustments may also be made on a flat sum or "across-the-board" basis, in which case a set amount is added to, or decreased from, all salaries on the schedule. The amount to be added or decreased is usually based on the percentage of fluctuation of the cost of living from the base schedule. There is a question as to what one salary on the schedule this percentage should be applied in order to arrive at the flat sum figure.

---

[12] Ibid., p.12.
[13] "Minimum Library Salary Standards for 1951," op. cit.
[14] These examples are taken from "Minimum Library Salary Standards for 1951," op. cit.

Examples:

As in the previous examples, a 45.6% increase is used for illustration, and this is applied to the beginning professional salary. This would add $957 to all salaries in the schedule.

(1) The $2100-$2580 range would be the same as above, or $3057-$3537.

(2) The $3450-$4290 range would be $4407-$5247.

(3) The $4800-$6000 range would be $5757-$6957.

Whichever plan is used, the ones charged with this duty must seek to devise the best means of assuring proper relationship of grades to each other and the most equitable and fair treatment to all.

With a basic salary schedule and a cost-of-living adjustment in operation, the employee advances by annual or periodic increments, if merited, until he reaches the maximum for his grade. Any cost-of-living adjustment should be granted to all, even though some may be at the maximum of their grades on the basic schedule or may not have merited the increment.

Adopting the Salary Schedule

Official adoption of the salary schedule by the governing body is necessary before it can go into operation. The chief librarian should present the plan, explaining how it was developed and how he believes it will aid in recruiting, improve staff morale, and reduce turnover. He will need to be armed with data such as facts concerning the rates of competing employers, salary standards, and cost-of-living figures for the local area. If possible, he should also present a tentative approval of the salary schedule from the employees. He must know what the annual salary budget would be under the plan, since the governing body cannot adopt it unless it can be financed in the budget. The resolution of adoption should state the effective date of the plan, and, in case any individual exceptions are to be made to the schedule, a statement providing for them should be included.

Placing the Classified Positions on the Scale

Once the salary schedule has been adopted, specific salaries are assigned to individual employees. In case the previous schedule was based on a classification of positions according to duties and responsibilities similar to the new plan, the transition is not difficult. The individual is placed on the same step of the new schedule as he was on the old. In practice the transition is usually not so simple, since the new plan generally has a somewhat different basis than the old.

Since the individual moves from the minimum to the maximum of the salary range for his grade from year to year through increased efficiency, employees should be placed on the new scale on the basis of satisfactory experience.

Example:

Such a plan as the following might be worked out:

Less than 1 complete year of experience - Minimum rate for the grade
1-2 years of satisfactory experience - Second step on the scale
2-3 years of satisfactory experience - Third step on the scale
3-4 years of satisfactory experience - Fourth step on the scale
4-5 years of satisfactory experience - Fifth step on the scale

In the case of the employee whose present compensation is in excess of the new maximum for his position, the recommended practice is to allow him to continue at his present salary. It should be clearly understood that his salary will remain at this figure as long as he remains in that position. In case cost-of-living increases occur later, he, of course, would receive the benefit of such increases. An effort should be made to transfer this individual to a position calling for a salary range in which his present pay rate would fall, but this is not always possible, since he may not meet the educational and personal requirements of such a position.

After individual salaries have been set, it is advisable to review with supervisors the salaries for positions under their supervision. Some revision may be necessary after these conferences.

The next step is to present the plan to the entire staff. Such a presentation should explain the basis of the new pay plan, how the rates were set, how the salary ranges were determined, what provision has been made for a career service, and how the cost of living influenced the schedule. A final step is to issue to each employee an appointment letter or form noting his classification grade and salary for the forthcoming year.

The question as to whether a list of individual salaries should be distributed or posted for the information of the entire staff should be a staff decision, providing there is no general administrative or board policy prohibiting it. The publication of allocation lists and the salary schedule revealed the class and salary range into which each position fell. The chief librarian should take the stand that individual salaries may be made public, but he should point out that those who receive no increase because of poor merit rating may not wish to have this fact made known.

Administering the Salary Schedule

Certain policies should be adopted concerning the administration of the salary schedule. A number of these have to do with the salary of new appointees. Under some civil service systems there is a ruling that all appointments must be made at the minimum salary of the grade. If credit for comparable experience in other libraries is allowed, such a policy must be determined with great care. No more than half credit is usually given for this outside experience.

Example:

Less than 2 complete years of experience - Minimum rate for the grade
2-4 years of satisfactory experience - Second step on the scale

      4-6 years of satisfactory experience - Third step on the scale
      6-8 years of satisfactory experience - Fourth step on the scale
      8-10 years of satisfactory experience - Fifth step on the scale

The final determination should be based on keeping a proper balance between the salary of the incoming employee and the salaries of those already on the staff. Morale can be quickly broken by bringing in a less experienced person at a higher rate than present staff members are receiving.

    A policy should also be adopted concerning the granting of increments. It has already been stated that increments should be given only on the basis of carefully prepared merit-rating sheets. There is also the question of how the length of service controls the granting of increments. The policy may be to give the first increment after the employee has completed six months of service in the grade, and subsequent increases are then granted on the anniversary of the date of this first increment. When only annual increments are given, they may be made on the anniversary of the individual's starting date or all granted on one date, usually the beginning of the calendar or fiscal year. If this latter plan is used, a policy must be determined as to the length of time the individual must have been in the grade in order to be eligible for the increment. It seems a fair policy to make the employee eligible if he has served at least six months during the preceding fiscal or calendar year.

    Some decision should also be made concerning the employee who has been on leave of absence for study, either for library training or for subject specialization. The policy may be to make him eligible for a salary increment at the normal time he would receive one, or a waiting period of a few months may be set up. During this waiting period, the work of the individual is closely observed, and if benefit from the study is noted, he then receives the increment. Policies concerning increments should also be made for employees on other leaves, such as for illness or sabbatical leave.

    A promotion to a position in a higher grade should always be accompanied by an increase to at least the minimum salary for that grade. A transfer from one position to another in the same grade is not usually accompanied by an increase in salary.

    All policies concerning the administration of the salary schedule should be put clearly in writing and should accompany the printed schedule.

Keeping the Salary Schedule Current

    Continuous revision of the salary schedule is tied in with the revision of the position-classification plan. When positions are reclassified, the salary attached to the new allocation should be granted. In case positions are created which require a new grade, a salary range must be determined in the same way that the original ranges were set.

    The true test of a salary schedule is in working with it. It may be discovered that inequities exist, that recruiting is difficult, or that promotion lines are not adequate. The classification plan should also be examined for any possible changes in qualification requirements or in class groupings which might affect the salary of individual positions. These corrections and any cost-of-living revisions should be made after a thorough review of the entire schedule. This is usually done on an annual basis at the time new budget figures are being assembled, as changes affect the total salary budget and must be dependent upon available funds. Just as it is recommended that the position-classification plan be revised at least every five years, it is also advisable to make a complete revision of the salary schedule at these stated intervals. All the steps in making a salary schedule should be taken exactly as they were in the original process.

The whole process of position classification and salary scheduling is technical, but if some outside help is available, it need not be too difficult for a library, large or small, to carry it out. Moreover, the attendant benefits of such a plan more than compensate for the work involved. The employee in the modern world is demanding "equal pay for equal work," and a job analysis resulting in a sound and workable classification plan is the only logical way in which such a demand can be met.

SUMMARY OF STEPS INVOLVED IN A
POSITION-CLASSIFICATION AND SALARY-ADMINISTRATION SURVEY

Planning and preparing for the survey	1.	Sell the idea to all concerned
	2.	Decide who is to head up and develop the program
	3.	Decide what positions are to be included in the survey
	4.	Select the method
	5.	Assemble and study the necessary tools
Conducting the survey	6.	Prepare the job analysis questionnaire
	7.	Prepare instructions to accompany the questionnaire
	8.	Arrange with supervisors for the analysis
	9.	Explain the survey plans to employees
	10.	Distribute the questionnaires to employees
	11.	Check in and arrange questionnaires
	12.	Write job descriptions
	13.	Hold interviews with employees and supervisors
	14.	Write job specifications
Selecting the factors	15.	Select the factors to be used in classifying positions
Analyzing positions and setting up a schedule of classes	16.	Analyze positions as to kind of work and level of responsibility
	17.	Determine classes
	18.	Select class titles
	19.	Write class definitions
	20.	Set up classification grades
	21.	Inform employees of tentative classification grades, class titles, and definitions
Ranking positions and assigning them to classes	22.	Tentatively allocate positions to classes
	23.	Write class specifications
	24.	Review and publish class specifications
	25.	Notify employees of their allocations
	26.	Adjust disagreements
Adopting the position-classification plan	27.	Secure approval from governing body for adoption of the plan
Installing and administering the plan	28.	Decide who is to install and administer the plan
	29.	Formulate rules under which the plan will operate
	30.	Reclassify positions when necessary
	31.	Review whole plan periodically
Preparing the salary schedule	32.	Decide who is to prepare and administer the schedule

33. Select the factors to be used in setting the schedule
34. Set a rate for key positions
35. Set rates for other positions with respect to key positions
36. Establish salary ranges for each grade
37. Provide for a career service
38. Provide for cost-of-living adjustments

Adopting the salary schedule

39. Secure approval from governing body for adoption of the schedule

Installing and administering the schedule

40. Place the classified positions on the schedule
41. Establish policies for administering the salary schedule
42. Review whole schedule periodically

SELECTED BIBLIOGRAPHY

American Library Association. Board on Personnel Administration. <u>Classification and Pay Plans for Municipal Public Libraries</u>. Chicago: American Library Assn., 1939. 189p.

_____ Board on Personnel Administration. Subcommittee on Analysis of Library Duties. <u>Descriptive List of Professional and Nonprofessional Duties in Libraries</u>. Preliminary draft. Chicago: American Library Assn., 1948. 75p.

_____ Board on Personnel Administration. Subcommittee on Budgets, Compensation and Schemes of Service for Libraries Connected with Universities, Colleges and Teacher Training Institutions. <u>Classification and Pay Plans for Libraries in Institutions of Higher Education</u>. 2d ed. Chicago: American Library Assn., 1947. 3v.

American Management Association. <u>Handbook of Business Administration</u>; W. J. Donald, editor-in-chief. N.Y.: McGraw-Hill, 1931. p.855-81, 1135-38.

Balderston, C. Canby. <u>Wage Setting Based on Job Analysis and Evaluation</u>. Industrial relations monograph, No. 4. N.Y.: Industrial Relations Counselors, 1940. 59p.

Baruch, Ismar. <u>Facts and Fallacies about Position-classification</u>. Pamphlet, No. 10. Chicago: Civil Service Assembly of the United States and Canada, November 1937. 25p.

Bryant, Douglas W., and Kaiser, Boynton S. "A University Library Position Classification and Compensation Plan," <u>Library Quarterly</u>, XVII (January 1947), 1-17.

Chicago. University. Graduate Library School. Library Institute. <u>Personnel Administration in Libraries</u>; papers presented before the Library Institute at the University of Chicago, August 27-September 1, 1945, edited with an introduction by Lowell Martin. Chicago: Univ. of Chicago Pr., c1946. 168p.

Civil Service Assembly of the United States and Canada. Committee on Position-classification and Pay Plans in the Public Service. <u>Position-classification in the Public Service</u>. Chicago: The Assembly, 1941. 404p.

Halsey, George D. <u>Handbook of Personnel Management</u>. N.Y.: Harper, c1947. p.11-45, 216-33.

Hitt, Eleanor. "Advantages of a Classified Service in Libraries," <u>Library Journal</u>, LXI (September 15, 1936), 663-66.

_____ "Classification and Pay Plans," <u>A.L.A. Bulletin</u>, XXXII (October 1, 1938), 697-702.

Hopwood, James O. <u>Salaries, Wages and Labor Relations</u>. Rev. ptg. N.Y.: Ronald Pr., [1945]. 128p.

McFadden, Marian, and Norris, Helen L. "A Case Study in Self Job Analysis," A.L.A. Bulletin, XL (November 1946), 436-40.

Mosher, William E., and Kingsley, J. Donald. Public Personnel Administration. Rev. ed. N.Y.: Harper, 1941. p.407-38.

"Newark Public Library's New Position Classification and Pay Plan," N.P.L. News, Supp. June 1945. p.49-68.

Otis, Jay L., and Leukart, Richard H. Job Evaluation; a basis for sound wage administration. N.Y.: Prentice-Hall, 1948. p.177-265.

Pffifner, John M. Public Administration. Rev. ed. N.Y.: Ronald Pr., [1946]. p.283-93.

Remley, Ralph D. "Position Classification in Administration," Library Journal, LXXI (June 1, and 15, 1946), 794-97, 856-58.

U. S. Bureau of Manpower Utilization. Occupational Analysis and Manning Tables Division. Training and Reference Manual for Job Analysis. Washington: War Manpower Commission, 1944. 104p.

Voorhies, Darrell H. "Job Analysis Is Organization's Tool," Library Journal, LXXII (December 15, 1947), 1737, 46-47; LXXIII (January 1, 1948), 33-35.

Appendix A

JOB ANALYSIS QUESTIONNAIRE

Please read instructions before filling out questionnaire

1. NAME _____ 2. DEPARTMENT or BRANCH _____

3. POSITION TITLE _____ 4. TOTAL HOURS PER WEEK _____

5. DAILY SCHEDULE (per week) _____

6. RATE OF PAY $_____ per (month, day, hour)

7. ADDITIONAL PAY _____
   (travel, living, overtime, etc.)

8. NAME AND TITLE OF YOUR SUPERVISOR (the person who assigns your work, gives you instructions, etc. If more than one, give name and title of each.)

_____

9. STATEMENT OF DUTIES
   This is the most important item on the questionnaire. List your regular tasks first, then your occasional tasks, and check (✔) occasional tasks. If more space is needed, use an additional sheet, and be sure your name is on the second sheet. Indicate in the left-hand column the percentage of time given to each task.

% of Time	TASKS

10. HOW LONG HAVE YOUR DUTIES AND DISTRIBUTION OF TIME BEEN SUBSTANTIALLY AS ITEMIZED IN QUESTION 9? _____

11. SUPERVISION RECEIVED
    a. How frequently do you receive assignments and instructions from your supervisor?

    b. Do these instructions cover all phases of your work?

    c. In what way is it necessary for you to use your own initiative in the performance of your work?

    d. Is your work reviewed while in process or upon completion by your supervisor or some other member of your department?

    e. Is your supervisor always, frequently, or infrequently available to review work and advise?

12. SUPERVISION OVER OTHERS
    Number supervised   Position titles of those supervised

    What is the nature of your supervision?

13. CERTIFICATE OF EMPLOYEE
    I hereby certify that the foregoing information supplied by me is correct as to fact, that it is expressed in my own words, and that it describes my job as I understand it.

DATE _____ SIGNATURE AND TITLE _____

14. CERTIFICATE OF IMMEDIATE SUPERVISOR
    I hereby certify that I have carefully considered the answers of this employee to the foregoing questions, and that to the best of my knowledge they are correct and complete as to facts within my knowledge, with the following exceptions:

DATE _____ SIGNATURE AND TITLE _____

15. CERTIFICATE OF DEPARTMENT CHIEF, BRANCH LIBRARIAN, OR CHIEF LIBRARIAN (If same as #14, do not sign.)
    I hereby certify that I have carefully considered the answers of this employee to the foregoing questions, and that to the best of my knowledge they are correct and complete as to facts within my knowledge, with the following exceptions:

DATE _____ SIGNATURE AND TITLE _____

Appendix B

DAILY WORK SHEET - DESK ASSISTANT

Smith, Jane
NAME

October 8, 1948
DATE

Circulation   Desk Assistant
DEPT. or BRANCH   POSITION TITLE

HOUR	TASKS PERFORMED	HOUR	TASKS PERFORMED
9-10	8:30-9 Morning routines - changed dates, sharpened pencils, counted and arranged circulation and entered in ledger 9-10 Looked up overdues on shelves, typed overdues	3-4	3-3:30 Book talk 3:30-3:50 Rest period 3:50-4 Desk - charged, etc.
10-11	10-10:15 Typed book cards 10:15-11 Looked up registration in files, checked on references, filed applications	4-5	4-5 Desk - charged, etc.
11-12	11-12 Desk - charged, took in and slipped books, registered borrowers, helped them find books	5-6	5-5:30 Desk - charged, etc.
12-1	Lunch	6-7	
1-2	1-2 Desk - charged, etc.	7-8	
2-3	2-3 Gave a book talk to P.T.A. group	8-9	

Appendix C

DAILY WORK SHEET - CHIEF, CIRCULATION DEPARTMENT

Jones, Mary
NAME

October 8, 1948

Circulation   Chief, Circulation Dept.   DATE
DEPT. or BRANCH   POSITION TITLE

HOUR	TASKS PERFORMED	HOUR	TASKS PERFORMED
9-10		3-4	Floor work - helped patrons find books, interviewed a woman about a study course
10-11		4-5	Floor work - helped patrons find books. Started making out a study course. Desk assistant asked advice on a matter of circulation policy
11-12		5-6	Supper
12-1	Worked on weekly desk schedule. Wrote letter to patron about long overdue book	6-7	Desk - charged, took in and slipped books, registered borrowers, helped them find books. Between times looked at book reviewing periodical for selection
1-2	1-1:30 Talked to desk assistant about reserve and overdue problems 1:30-2 Worked on shelves taking off books to bind, mend, or discard	7-8	Desk - charged, etc.
2-3	Worked on shelves - binds, mends, discards Checked on shelving of page Called from stacks to handle a circulation complaint	8-9	Desk - charged, etc.

Appendix D

SAMPLE INSTRUCTIONS

Nature and Objectives of the Survey

A fundamental requirement of sound administrative management in any organization is an orderly, systematic grouping of all the positions in the organization into what is known as a POSITION-CLASSIFICATION PLAN. Such a plan is ordinarily based on a thorough, objective study of each position as it exists at the moment, known as a JOB ANALYSIS. The greatest single factor in this analysis is the employee's own verified statement of his duties, furnished in accordance with the procedure set forth in these instructions.

Information obtained from a classification study provides a more intelligent approach to all phases of personnel management: in establishing an equitable pay plan; in recruiting and testing, promotion and transfer, training and rating employees; in planning and improving organization; and in promoting better employee-management relations.

Purpose of Questionnaire

The facts about the duties performed in any given position are best known to the employee on the job. The questionnaire seeks the employee's version of his duties and responsibilities.

This form is your unrestricted opportunity to describe your job as you see it. Make every effort to record every distinct duty and every element of responsibility which you know the job entails. Your own version of the work you do, unhampered by any suggestion or influence of anyone else, is the information sought. Your immediate supervisor, and your department chief, branch librarian, or the chief librarian will be permitted to see your statement and to comment on it, but they will not be permitted to change it. If it appears that there are conflicting ideas about what you do, a full investigation will be made to establish the real facts.

Please bear in mind that the important facts are the DUTIES AND RESPONSIBILITIES. Lengthy descriptions of other factors are of no value for the particular purposes of this survey.

How to Fill Out the Form

With these instructions you will have received a set of two copies of the questionnaire, on which items 1, 2, 3, and 6 have already been filled out.

Before you do anything to the questionnaire, please:

1. Study all of these instructions until you are sure you understand them.
2. Study the questionnaire carefully.
3. Prepare a draft of your answers <u>on a separate sheet of paper</u>.

The Following Instructions Should Aid You in Preparing Your Answers:

<u>Item 4</u>. Show the total number of hours you normally work in a week.

<u>Item 5</u>. Show the actual hours within which you ordinarily do your work. For example: 4 days, 8:00 - 5:00; 1 day, 12:00 - 9:00. If your schedule is irregular, give schedule for the <u>current</u> week.

<u>Item 7</u>. If living or travel expenses are allowed over and above your basic rate, indicate what expenses are allowed. If overtime pay is given, indicate rate and frequency. List any other allowances.

<u>Item 8</u>. Give the name and title of your immediate supervisor; that is, the person to whom you go for assignments, advice, and decisions. If you have more than one supervisor to whom you regularly report and from whom you regularly receive instructions, give the name and title of each.

<u>Item 9</u>. The answer to this item requires an exact, detailed account of what you do. Explain briefly, but carefully, each task you perform, listing your regular tasks first.

Be specific in describing your tasks. For example, if one of your tasks is typing, state briefly what kind of things you type and where, and under what conditions. If your work involves the preparation of reports, indicate the kinds, the purpose of each, and exactly what you contribute to them. Such expressions as "filing," "keeping records," "assisting in the preparation of reports" are of little value unless we know the type of files and the kinds of filing, the kind and purpose of the records, the kind and purpose of the reports, and, in each case, exactly what you contribute.

In the left-hand column indicate what percentage of your time is spent at each task which you perform. Figure percentage of time on a weekly basis. For example, you may spend 20 hours of a 40-hour week in charging and discharging books. If so, 50% should be recorded in the left-hand column before that particular task. Or, you may spend two hours of a 40-hour week in compiling bibliographies or filing borrowers' applications. If so, 5% should appear before that particular task. A percentage estimate must appear before each task. Fractions of percentages should not be used, thus the total may be slightly short of 100%, but it should approximate it.

If periodic tasks (those performed at recurring fixed intervals, such as monthly and annual reports) amount to 1% or more of the total <u>annual</u> time, list them after the regular tasks with the percentage of time spent. Annual time is figured on the basis of total hours worked per year. Occasional tasks are those performed irregularly, usually in times of emergency, and should only be checked (✓) and no percentage of time given.

<u>Item 11</u>. Answer these questions specifically and briefly.
   (a) Indicate that assignments and instructions are given several times a day as new work is given, daily, weekly, or other specified time.
   (b) If these instructions do not cover all phases of the work, indicate what areas are left to your own discretion.

(c) Give specific examples of the use of your own initiative.
(d) Indicate who reviews your work and the usual frequency of that review.
(e) Indicate the availability of your supervisor to give you advice and to review your work.

Item 12. Answer this item only if you are actually responsible for the work of others. Mere inspection, checking or proofreading do not in themselves constitute supervision or direction. If you do assign and direct the work of others, list the number supervised and the titles of their positions. If your supervision over certain employees is shared with another supervisor, indicate that fact, showing the division of authority, and giving the name of the other supervisor. Indicate the nature and amount of supervision in regard to the giving of assignments and instructions, revision of work, etc.

When you are sure that the answers you have recorded on the separate sheet are complete and accurate, type them, or have them typed, on the questionnaire.

Item 13. Your certification to the statements on the questionnaire is required. After certifying each copy and dating it, give both copies to your immediate supervisor. The carbon copy will be returned to you later.

The completed questionnaire must be given to your supervisor within five days from the time you receive it.

Items 14 & 15. The questionnaire is to be reviewed and signed by your supervisors in turn and passed on within one week of the date received.

The immediate supervisor may be a departmental assistant, a department chief, a branch librarian, or even the chief librarian. Whatever the title, the person who has the most direct supervision over the position should sign here.

Item 15 provides for the signature of the supervisor who is one step removed from the supervision of this position. If a branch librarian has signed Item 14, the chief librarian may be the one to sign here. If the chief librarian is the immediate supervisor, this space should remain blank.

Appendix E

COMPLETED JOB ANALYSIS QUESTIONNAIRE - DESK ASSISTANT

Please read instructions before filling out questionnaire

1. NAME __Smith, Jane__   2. DEPARTMENT or BRANCH __Circulation__

3. POSITION TITLE __Desk Assistant__   4. TOTAL HOURS PER WEEK __40__

5. DAILY SCHEDULE (per week) __2 days, 8:30-5:30; 1 day, 9-6; 2 days, 12-9__

6. RATE OF PAY $ __175__ per (month✓, day, hour)

7. ADDITIONAL PAY __None__
   (travel, living, overtime, etc.)

8. NAME AND TITLE OF YOUR SUPERVISOR (the person who assigns your work, gives you instructions, etc. If more than one, give name and title of each.)

   Mary Jones, Chief, Circulation Department

---

9. STATEMENT OF DUTIES

   This is the most important item on the questionnaire. List your regular tasks first, then your occasional tasks, and check (✓) occasional tasks. If more space is needed, use an additional sheet, and be sure your name is on the second sheet. Indicate in the left-hand column the percentage of time given to each task.

% of Time	TASKS
50	Charging, taking in and slipping books, registering borrowers, helping patrons to find books
15	Registration - looking up applications and references, making out new cards, filing applications, pulling expired registration
10	Looking up overdues on shelves and writing notices
10	Looking for reserves on shelves and in circulation, telephoning patrons
5	Setting up displays of books
3	Book talks
1	Typing book cards
1	Morning routines - changing daters, sharpening pencils, counting and arranging circulation and entering in ledger
5	Rest period and unaccounted for time
100	
✓	Telling stories to children in absence of children's librarian

10. HOW LONG HAVE YOUR DUTIES AND DISTRIBUTION OF TIME BEEN SUBSTANTIALLY AS ITEMIZED IN QUESTION 9? __10 months__

11. SUPERVISION RECEIVED
    a. How frequently do you receive assignments and instructions from your supervisor?
       Assignments made in daily work schedule. Instructions given rarely, only when a new job is to be done.
    b. Do these instructions cover all phases of your work? Yes.
    c. In what way is it necessary for you to use your own initiative in the performance of your work?
       In helping patrons, I have to know where to look for the requested material.
    d. Is your work reviewed while in process or upon completion by your supervisor or some other member of your department? No.
    e. Is your supervisor always, frequently, or infrequently available to review work and advise? Frequently.

12. SUPERVISION OVER OTHERS
    Number supervised   Position titles of those supervised

    None.

    What is the nature of your supervision?

13. CERTIFICATE OF EMPLOYEE
    I hereby certify that the foregoing information supplied by me is correct as to fact, that it is expressed in my own words, and that it describes my job as I understand it.

    DATE __October 19, 1948__   SIGNATURE AND TITLE __Jane Smith, Desk Assistant__

14. CERTIFICATE OF IMMEDIATE SUPERVISOR
    I hereby certify that I have carefully considered the answers of this employee to the foregoing questions, and that to the best of my knowledge they are correct and complete as to facts within my knowledge, with the following exceptions:

    DATE __October 25, 1948__   SIGNATURE AND TITLE __Mary Jones, Chief, Circulation__
                                                                              Department

15. CERTIFICATE OF DEPARTMENT HEAD, BRANCH LIBRARIAN, OR CHIEF LIBRARIAN (If same as #14, do not sign.)
    I hereby certify that I have carefully considered the answers of this employee to the foregoing questions, and that to the best of my knowledge they are correct and complete as to facts within my knowledge, with the following exceptions:

    DATE __October 29, 1948__   SIGNATURE AND TITLE __Ann Brown, Chief Librarian__

Appendix F

COMPLETED JOB ANALYSIS QUESTIONNAIRE – CHIEF, CIRCULATION DEPARTMENT

Please read instructions before filling out questionnaire

1. NAME Jones, Mary   2. DEPARTMENT or BRANCH Circulation
3. POSITION TITLE Chief, Circulation Dept.   4. TOTAL HOURS PER WEEK 40
5. DAILY SCHEDULE (per week) 3 days, 9-6; 2 days, 12-9
6. RATE OF PAY $ 275 per (month, day, hour)
7. ADDITIONAL PAY None
                          (travel, living, overtime, etc.)
8. NAME AND TITLE OF YOUR SUPERVISOR (the person who assigns your work, gives you instructions, etc. If more than one, give name and title of each.)

   Ann Brown, Chief Librarian

9. STATEMENT OF DUTIES

   This is the most important item on the questionnaire. List your regular tasks first, then your occasional tasks, and check (✓) occasional tasks. If more space is needed, use an additional sheet, and be sure your name is on the second sheet. Indicate in the left-hand column the percentage of time given to each task.

% of Time	TASKS
30	Helping patrons with requests
15	Supervising work of the department, making schedules
15	Desk routine – charging, discharging, slipping
10	Sorting books for binding, mending, discarding
10	Book selection
5	Book talks
5	Making book lists
5	Writing publicity
5 / 100	Rest periods and unaccounted for time
✓	Taking book inventory (every third year)
2% yearly	Making monthly and annual reports

10. HOW LONG HAVE YOUR DUTIES AND DISTRIBUTION OF TIME BEEN SUBSTANTIALLY AS ITEMIZED IN QUESTION 9? 2½ years

11. SUPERVISION RECEIVED
    a. How frequently do you receive assignments and instructions from your supervisor?
       Rarely. The work is set up, and changes are made only after consultation with the chief librarian.
    b. Do these instructions cover all phases of your work?
       In a general way, yes. Few specific instructions.
    c. In what way is it necessary for you to use your own initiative in the performance of your work?
       In almost every task initiative is needed.
    d. Is your work reviewed while in process or upon completion by your supervisor or some other member of your department? No.
    e. Is your supervisor always, frequently, or infrequently available to review work and advise? Frequently.

12. SUPERVISION OVER OTHERS

    Number supervised   Position titles of those supervised
    3   Desk Assistants
    1 (part time)   Page

    What is the nature of your supervision?
    I give assignments in the daily work schedules and give instructions when needed. Do not usually review work, but am available to give advice in regard to policies or routines.

13. CERTIFICATE OF EMPLOYEE
    I hereby certify that the foregoing information supplied by me is correct as to fact, that it is expressed in my own words, and that it describes my job as I understand it.

DATE October 18, 1948   SIGNATURE AND TITLE Mary Jones, Chief,
                                                Circulation Department

14. CERTIFICATE OF IMMEDIATE SUPERVISOR
    I hereby certify that I have carefully considered the answers of this employee to the foregoing questions, and that to the best of my knowledge they are correct and complete as to facts within my knowledge, with the following exceptions:

DATE October 25, 1948   SIGNATURE AND TITLE Ann Brown, Chief Librarian

15. CERTIFICATE OF DEPARTMENT HEAD, BRANCH LIBRARIAN, OR CHIEF LIBRARIAN (If same as #14, do not sign.)
    I hereby certify that I have carefully considered the answers of this employee to the foregoing questions, and that to the best of my knowledge they are correct and complete as to facts within my knowledge, with the following exceptions:

DATE _____ SIGNATURE AND TITLE _____

Appendix G

COMPLETED JOB ANALYSIS QUESTIONNAIRE – JUNIOR REFERENCE LIBRARIAN

Please read instructions before filling out questionnaire

1. NAME __Green, Sue__ 2. DEPARTMENT or BRANCH __Reference__

3. POSITION TITLE __Junior Reference Librarian__ 4. TOTAL HOURS PER WEEK __40__

5. DAILY SCHEDULE (per week) __3 days, 9-6; 2 days, 12-9__

6. RATE OF PAY $ __225__ per (m̄onth, day, hour)

7. ADDITIONAL PAY __None__
   (travel, living, overtime, etc.)

8. NAME AND TITLE OF YOUR SUPERVISOR (the person who assigns your work, gives you instructions, etc. If more than one, give name and title of each.)

   Dorothy Black, Chief, Reference Department

9. STATEMENT OF DUTIES

   This is the most important item on the questionnaire. List your regular tasks first, then your occasional tasks, and check (✓) occasional tasks. If more space is needed, use an additional sheet, and be sure your name is on the second sheet. Indicate in the left-hand column the percentage of time given to each task.

% of Time	TASKS
60	Answering reference questions – includes getting magazines, city and telephone directories, newspapers and government documents from the stacks
10	Ordering, checking in, and filing government documents
10	Assigning subject headings, filing and weeding pamphlet and picture files
5	Clipping newspapers and magazines, assigning subject headings, and filing material in clipping files and indexes
5	Making bibliographies
5	Handling interlibrary loans
5	Rest periods and unaccounted for time
100	
✓	Giving instruction to school classes in use of catalog, Readers' Guide, etc. in absence of chief of department

10. HOW LONG HAVE YOUR DUTIES AND DISTRIBUTION OF TIME BEEN SUBSTANTIALLY AS ITEMIZED IN QUESTION 9? <u>18 months</u>

11. SUPERVISION RECEIVED
    a. How frequently do you receive assignments and instructions from your supervisor?
       Rarely. General instructions were given when I started the job, and additional ones are made occasionally. No specific assignments as we take the patrons in turn.
    b. Do these instructions cover all phases of your work?
       General instructions only in regard to policy, files, etc.
    c. In what way is it necessary for you to use your own initiative in the performance of your work?
       Initiative used in every reference question handled.
    d. Is your work reviewed while in process or upon completion by your supervisor or some other member of your department?
       Not usually. Some subject heading work and bibliographies occasionally checked by chief of department.
    e. Is your supervisor always, frequently, or infrequently available to review work and advise?
       Frequently. Because of staggered schedules, she is not always at hand.

12. SUPERVISION OVER OTHERS
    Number supervised   Position titles of those supervised
         None.
    What is the nature of your supervision?

13. CERTIFICATE OF EMPLOYEE
    I hereby certify that the foregoing information supplied by me is correct as to fact, that it is expressed in my own words, and that it describes my job as I understand it.

DATE <u>October 15, 1948</u>   SIGNATURE AND TITLE <u>Sue Green,</u>
                                                    Junior Reference Librarian

14. CERTIFICATE OF IMMEDIATE SUPERVISOR
    I hereby certify that I have carefully considered the answers of this employee to the foregoing questions, and that to the best of my knowledge they are correct and complete as to facts within my knowledge, with the following exceptions:

DATE <u>October 20, 1948</u>   SIGNATURE AND TITLE <u>Dorothy Black, Chief,</u>
                                                    Reference Department

15. CERTIFICATE OF DEPARTMENT HEAD, BRANCH LIBRARIAN, OR CHIEF LIBRARIAN (If same as #14, do not sign.)
    I hereby certify that I have carefully considered the answers of this employee to the foregoing questions, and that to the best of my knowledge they are correct and complete as to facts within my knowledge, with the following exceptions:

DATE <u>October 25, 1948</u>   SIGNATURE AND TITLE <u>Ann Brown, Chief Librarian</u>

Appendix H

SAMPLE JOB DESCRIPTION - DESK ASSISTANT[1]

1. Job Title - Desk Assistant

2. Job Summary - Under the general supervision of the Chief of the Circulation Department, to assist with the general work of the department.

3. Work Performed

Per Cent of Time	Tasks
40%	Issuing, renewing, receiving and discharging books, registering borrowers
15	Maintaining registration files
10	Assisting readers to locate and select books
10	Issuing overdue notices
10	Reserving books
5	Planning and arranging bulletin boards and displays
3	Giving talks on books and reading
1	Typing filled book cards
1	Setting up the desk
5	Rest periods and unproductive time
100%	
Irregular duty	Planning and conducting story hours

[1] As revised after the interview described on p. 14-15.

Appendix I

SAMPLE JOB DESCRIPTION - CHIEF, CIRCULATION DEPARTMENT

1. Job Title - Chief, Circulation Department

2. Job Summary - Under the general direction of the Chief Librarian, to have charge of the work of the Circulation Department and supervise the staff of three full-time members and a part-time page.

3. Work Performed

Per Cent of Time	Tasks
20%	Assisting readers to locate and select books
10	Individual reading guidance
5	Giving talks on books and reading
5	Compiling and distributing reading lists
5	Supervising order and appearance of shelves, shifting books
10	Sorting and making final decisions on items to be bound, mended, or discarded
5	Supervising loan procedures, overdues, reserves, handling complaints
5	Selecting books for purchase
5	Preparing lists of material needed in specific subjects
15	Issuing, renewing, receiving and discharging books, registering borrowers
5	Preparing work and time schedules
5	Planning and writing news stories and articles
5	Rest periods and unproductive time
100%	
Irregular duty	Planning, supervising and taking book inventory every third year
2% yearly	Compiling monthly and annual statistics

Appendix J

SAMPLE JOB DESCRIPTION - JUNIOR REFERENCE LIBRARIAN

1. Job Title - Junior Reference Librarian

2. Job Summary - Under the general supervision of the Chief of the Reference Department, to assist with the technical reference work of the department.

3. Work Performed

Per Cent of Time	Tasks
60%	Answering reference questions
10	Ordering, checking in, and filing government documents
10	Organizing and maintaining information files
5	Making special indexes
5	Compiling bibliographies
5	Verifying bibliographical data for interlibrary loans and keeping these records
5	Rest periods and unproductive time
100%	
Irregular duty	Instruction in reference sources and methods in absence of chief of department

Appendix K

SAMPLE CLASS SPECIFICATION

CHIEF CIRCULATION LIBRARIAN[1]
Class A Circulation Department

Definition of the Class of Position:

Under direction of the Chief Librarian or the Associate (or Assistant) Chief Librarian, to have charge of the work of a Class A Circulation Department, i.e., having a staff of 2 to 6 full-time members (or their equivalent in part time) including the chief; and to do such other work as may be required.

Examples of Typical Tasks:

Laying out and assigning the circulation and related work for the members of the Circulation Department staff and seeing that they are effectively employed; giving them directions and suggestions and aiding them with their difficult problems; developing the circulation procedure to meet the needs of the institution; helping readers or seeing that they are assisted in the selection of books and in the use of the catalog; keeping informed on needs of faculty members and students and acquainting them with available material; personally handling difficult situations with the faculty and students and adjusting complaints; supervising the work with reserves and interlibrary loans; directing the work of book shelving and stack maintenance; supervising the taking of inventory; reading and appraising books and other materials and making recommendations for their acquisition; making recommendations and decisions in matters of circulation policy; maintaining a manual of circulation routines; seeing that essential records and statistics are kept; preparing reports and memoranda; handling correspondence; preparing work schedules for the members of the staff; consulting with chiefs of departments; making recommendations regarding appointments, promotions, transfers, salary adjustments, and other personnel matters; rating staff members on their efficiency; developing the latent abilities of staff members and in general promoting staff esprit de corps; keeping in touch with library developments by attending conferences and reading professional literature; participating in campus activities.

Minimum Qualifications:

Professional: Education and experience as specified in Professional Grade 3; wide knowledge of circulation procedure and problems; good knowledge of

---

[1] This specification has been taken from American Library Association, Board on Personnel Administration, Subcommittee on Budgets, Compensation and Schemes of Service for Libraries Connected with Universities, Colleges and Teacher Training Institutions, Classification and Pay Plans for Libraries in Institutions of Higher Education (2d ed.; Chicago: American Library Assn., 1947), Vol. 3, Universities, p.47.

modern library organization, procedure, policy, aims, and service, particularly as they relate to circulation work; ability to use catalogs, bibliographies, book lists, and indexes; good knowledge of books; reading knowledge of one or more foreign languages and some familiarity with the literature of these languages; ability to organize and direct a Circulation Department; appreciation of the objectives and procedures of higher education.

Personal: Awareness of community; capacity for leadership; cooperativeness; good judgment; initiative; intellectual curiosity; orderliness, poise; resourcefulness; sense of humor; tact; ability to organize work; ability to direct, train, and supervise; ability to size up situations and people accurately, to get along well with faculty, superiors, co-workers, and subordinates and to meet the public pleasantly; ability to judge personnel.

Appendix L

SAMPLE CLASS SPECIFICATION

<u>INTERMEDIATE REFERENCE LIBRARIAN</u>[1]
Reference Department

Definition of the Class of Position:

Under supervision of the Chief Reference Librarian or other designated authority, to do reference work of average difficulty and responsibility and of a character calling for the application of modern library techniques; and to do such other work as may be required.

Examples of Typical Tasks:

Handling reference matters of average difficulty; giving instruction in the use of the library; working in the reference, bibliography, documents and periodicals reading rooms, and any other rooms under the jurisdiction of the Reference Department; compiling indexes, lists, and bibliographies; assisting with the technical work in the department; keeping essential records and statistics; supervising and revising the work of library clerks; keeping in touch with library developments by attending conferences and reading professional literature; participating in campus activities.

Minimum Qualifications:

Professional: Education and experience as specified in Professional Grade 2; working knowledge of reference procedure and problems and of the uses of catalogs, bibliographies, book lists, and indexes; knowledge of modern library organization, procedure, policy, aims, and service, particularly as they relate to reference work; knowledge of books and other reference materials; reading knowledge of one or more foreign languages; ability to do reference work of average difficulty; teaching ability; appreciation of the objectives and procedures of higher education.

Personal: Accuracy; cooperativeness; good judgment; intellectual curiosity; orderliness; poise; resourcefulness; sense of humor; tact; ability to follow instructions; ability to supervise; ability to get along well with faculty, superiors, co-workers, and subordinates and to meet the public pleasantly.

---

[1] This specification has been taken from American Library Association, Board on Personnel Administration, Subcommittee on Budgets, Compensation and Schemes of Service for Libraries Connected with Universities, Colleges and Teacher Training Institutions, <u>Classification and Pay Plans for Libraries in Institutions of Higher Education</u> (2d ed.; Chicago: American Library Assn., 1947), Vol. 3, Universities, p. 97.